SPARKLING WATERS

Peggy Burton

Publishers :

King's Highway Books
P.O. Box 789
Sutton Coldfield
West Midlands
B73 5FX
ENGLAND

Publishers :
King's Highway Books
P.O. Box 789
Sutton Coldfield
West Midlands
B73 5FX
ENGLAND

Further information or more copies can be obtained from :
King's Highway Books
P.O. Box 789
Sutton Coldfield
West Midlands
B73 5FX
ENGLAND

ISBN 0-9541015-7-X

© Front cover photograph by Tony Salter - Galápagos Island
Designed by: World Action Ministries
Printed by : Selsey Press Ltd, 84 High Street, Selsey, Chichester, West Sussex PO20 0QH Tel:01243 605234

CONTENTS

FOREWORD

It's a real delight and privilege to be invited to write this foreword for "Sparkling Waters," Peggy Burton's new book of daily thoughts and prayers. There are numerous books available on the Christian market to day that encourage us to read and study the Scriptures each day. How often though, do you hear good Christian people say that they just haven't been able to keep up the pace! Good intentions have so easily given way to the pressures of everyday life and the time given to daily Bible Study has suffered!

This is a special book and one that I can almost guarantee that you will still want to pick up and read at some point in your day, whatever is your habit, way on to the end of the year. You will never tire of Peggy's brief thoughts, the application, the scriptures she has chosen and the prayers that she encourages you to bring to the Lord each day.

Having read the whole manuscript through from beginning to end I can highly commend this to you as an excellent supplement to your daily spiritual intake. The Word of God is essential for us to grow and develop our Christian lives. This little book is based on nothing but God's Word.

Read, enjoy, be challenged, encouraged and blessed through these inspired pages written so effectively by one of God's chosen and faithful servants.

Philip B South
Director – World Action Ministries
September 2005

ACKNOWLEDGEMENTS

This book would certainly not have been ready this year unless James, my faithful husband, had not come to my rescue. As time was running out, without further ado, he offered to check all my work and also offered to help with the selection of suitable Scripture verses. This had proved extremely time consuming, finding the appropriate verses for my daily thoughts. What a wonderful help this has been, enabling the book to be ready on schedule.

Mike, our son-in-law, took control of the computer when it misbehaved. Somehow, it always listened to his instructions, but not always to mine! What would I have done without this help?

Thank you too, Phil South, Director of World Action Ministries, for writing a foreword for the book. Now we trust that the finished product will help to support some of the wonderful ministry that you supervise.

PREFACE

The object of this daily reading book is to encourage and challenge you to read one or two brief Scripture passages to start the day. They are applicable in any version of the Scriptures.

A few thoughts have been prepared to link into these Scripture references on a variety of subjects, with which we are all familiar. I hope they will inspire you.

We all have queries and doubts as we go through life, and most of us are confronted with problems, sickness, disappointments or sorrow at some time or other. But, guided by the Holy Spirit, I have tried to be helpful in my words and suggestions.

So I trust and pray that many of these thoughts and Scriptures will really be meaningful and helpful for you in your daily walk with the Lord.

———————

JANUARY

Deuteronomy 33v27   Ecclesiastes 8v7   Jeremiah 29v11-13

When people emigrate to a new country, they are going into an entirely new situation and are literally on the verge of the unknown. They go in expectation of what lies ahead.

Today you are entering upon a new year and you are standing on the edge of the unknown. What is the first thing you think about. Do you make New Year resolutions? Do you think about new experiences, changes and needs that might arise? At the start of this year you should place your life at God's disposal. Put your hands into His hands, trust Him to lead you and by faith know that He understands how you feel. He has already planned a way ahead for you. May this be a happy New Year in every sense.

PRAYER – Father, I want to enter this new year confident that I am following the way you have in mind for me. My resolution is to walk with Jesus all the way.

✓ JANUARY 2nd

Isaiah 55v8-13   Matthew 13v31-32   1Peter 1v23-25

The beginning of the year resembles the time when the seed that the farmer has planted is beginning to stir. The farmer has good intentions but he cannot know for certain how the seed will develop.

You cannot see into the future but you can have faith to believe that your thought seeds will develop according to God's will. Do you have good ideas, intentions and thoughts for things to develop this year? Spend time in God's presence and do what He asks you to do. Water the seed and go forward in faith, then expect the seed to grow and develop as you stay close to the Lord. Trust and obey, for there is no other way.

PRAYER – Father, I have so many thoughts going through my head at the beginning of this new year. Please help me to grow the right thought seeds in the right places, so that I may fit into Your plans.

JANUARY 3rd

Matthew 18v3-4   Matthew 28v20b   1John 3v1-3

Babies are unable to do things for themselves. They need care and attention and training, then as they develop and grow they are able to do more. Left on their own they would never survive.

Do you ever stop to consider that in your Christian life you are like a baby? You will never develop your Christian life unless you are trained and helped through your study of the Scriptures, together with Christian fellowship and teaching. Mature Christians can advise and guide, but you need Jesus in your life; He has promised never to leave you, so depend on His presence always.

PRAYER – Father, I look to You for care and protection and instructions. Thank you that You sent Jesus to help and guide me during my earthly pilgrimage. Please help me to constantly turn to Him in my daily needs.

JANUARY 4th

Psalm 139v11-12   Isaiah 60v20   1John 1v5-7

There is a wonderful sense of anticipation as darkness gives way to light when a new day dawns. Sometimes beautiful colours adorn the sky and one feels elated. At other times the whole scene is shrouded in cloud and mist and one tends to feel less elated.

God planned day and night for a purpose but there are times when the day seems to be immersed in darkness, with difficult decisions, sickness and occasions you do not understand. Problems don't always fade away and the way ahead seems clouded, but at least the light of God penetrates to assure you of His presence. At other times the light is clear and colourful and your heart should be full of praise. Do you have these experiences in various situations?

PRAYER – Father, thank you that as I look to You I can be assured that at the start of each new day You are there whatever the circumstances. I praise You for the light of Your life in my life.

JANUARY 5th

Psalm 102v25   Matthew 7v25   1Corinthians 3v11-15

When a building is designed it has to be planned. The beginning of a structure has to start with foundations. The whole building relies on a firm foundation.

As you think back to the early days of your faith in God, did you have a good foundation? In the Christian life the beginning is very important. You need to seek God's help so that the future will benefit from training and sound planning. You may have experienced difficulties and problems that have been hard to understand, but you must realise that God has a purpose in all eventualities in your life. He longs for you to build your foundation on Jesus, your Teacher and Leader.

PRAYER – Father, I need to develop my walk on the Christian way. I thank You for Your discipline and Your training programme, so that my life may grow and develop with a firm foundation on Jesus.

JANUARY 6th

Acts 20v24   1Corinthians 9v24-27   Hebrews 12v1-3

When a race is run the contestants have to line up at the starting point and wait for the signal to go. Then as the runners start they advance and it soon becomes obvious who has had good training.

Life is like a race. You line up at the starting point and wait for the 'on your mark' signal from God. Have you ever had this experience, lining up at the starting point, tense and anxious, looking towards the winning line and wondering if you can make it? Then 'off'. Go for it and keep your eyes on the goal. There will be 'hiccups' along the way but these will all be times when previous training will enable you to face up to the problem or difficulty, then be able to carry on. Your ultimate goal will be the Kingdom of Heaven and even the thought of that glorious goal should enable you to run with determination in the race set before you.

PRAYER – Father, thank You that it is possible for me to run the race You have set before me. Help me not to look back but to keep my eyes on Jesus all the way to my eventual goal.

JANUARY 7th

Genesis 1v1-31   Ecclesiastes 3v11   John 1v1-5

When we read a book we will most certainly start at page 1. As the story unfolds, we are anxious to know how the characters face up to the events ahead. So we will enthusiastically read on.

When you were first introduced to the Bible, did you want to read on so that you could know what happened to the characters as the story moved on? It is very important that you should spend time studying God's Word, because it is not always easy to understand. But as Christians we have the wonderful privilege of being able to know that God will make it clear to us when we ask Him to do so.

PRAYER – Father, thank You for Your Word. Please help me to understand the difficult parts and give me the desire to spend time in the truths that are revealed each day.

JANUARY 8th

Genesis 2v10-14   Psalm 46v4   Revelation 22v1-6

At the source of any river is a tiny outlet. Then as water flows it expands and flows as a mountain stream, developing as it goes, often splitting into several branches until it becomes a mighty river.

The Christian life should flow freely as it develops, pouring out the love of Christ and proclaiming His love in all you say and do. Where are you in your Christian life. Are you flowing freely or are you still in the mountain stream? You will often flow over rocks and stones and sometimes over a waterfall. Do not give up but be determined. Consider the help a river can be to so many in a variety of ways. Water is life saving so be encouraged.

PRAYER – Father, thank you for Your encouragement when I have doubts. May I keep going, realising that You rely on my part to witness amongst those who need what I am able to give.

JANUARY 9th

Philippians 3v12-14   Philippians 4v13   2Timothy 1v9

How does a little bird manage to fly as it leaves the nest? It has been fed and cared for by the mother bird, then as the moment arrives, she encourages and sometimes pushes the youngster to the edge of the nest. It topples into the air and by instinct, opens its tiny wings and flies!

There comes a time when you will know that God is encouraging you to 'take off'. Have you come to that point in your life and have you taken the plunge? You may hesitate, but the Lord has a task for you to do. He has nurtured you and now is the time to move on. Do not ignore the way God is calling you, but go forward and be assured that God will guide you all the way.

PRAYER – Father, I am so conscious of Your call but yet I hesitate as I view the future ahead. Help me to take courage. Thank you for Your loving care.

JANUARY 10th

Job 5v17   Proverbs 3v11-12   Hebrews 12v1-11

Cake making must be done according to the recipe. In some cases it is necessary to beat certain ingredients together. If this is not done correctly, the cake will be flat and uninteresting.

As you look into your Christian life are you following a recipe and preparing for the future? Maybe your life needs to be well beaten if you are to be a success, able to follow and serve the Lord as He wishes you to do. Be prepared for whatever treatment He considers necessary and then rejoice at the outcome. Think of the end results and never doubt instructions from the Lord.

PRAYER – Father, I am so hesitant when it comes to anything out of the ordinary. I like to follow my own ideas. Help me to realise that You have a reason for every occasion I experience.

JANUARY 11th

Matthew 3v3   1Corinthians 2v9-15   1Peter 1v13-16

The first thing we do in the morning when we wake up is to wash and dress. It is a routine that comes naturally. Would you consider going out in your nightwear unless for an emergency?

As you seek to follow the Lord into the programme He has for you in life, you will need to prepare yourself by 'putting on' the right attire. Take off the things that would hinder, that are not applicable or appear incorrect in your daily walk with Him. Be cleansed and ready in every situation to go forth in the joy of the Lord to serve Him faithfully.

PRAYER – Father, help me to realise how necessary it is for me to be prepared for the day ahead. Thank you for Your Word, Your love and Your guidance.

JANUARY 12th

John 9v4-5   Acts 20v24   1John 2v3-6

When it comes to mending a hole in a garment, we have to darn it with a needle and thread. This operation needs a certain amount of concentration as the hole is slowly filled and secured.

Do you have a hole in your life that needs to be repaired? In a sense, your place in life is like a hole and as you face it you have to concentrate and have the right 'tools' to tackle the task of filling up the hole. Spend time in prayer and in the study of God's Word. Jesus had a big hole to fill as He lived amongst people, seeking to lead them and teach them. He showed the way to salvation and in due course the hole was filled. He gave His life to save the world. His work was complete.

PRAYER – Father, I want to be complete in Jesus. Please give me the ability to fill up the holes in my life through the power of Your Holy Spirit.

JANUARY 13th

Job 5v17-18   Proverbs 6v23   John 8v34-36

The common cold will develop into a more serious condition unless it is controlled. Also it can be passed on to others to cause them trouble too.

Sin is like the common cold. If it is not dealt with in the beginning it will cause a lot of damage and can give more and more trouble as it develops. If you have a problem do you deal with it immediately or does it tend to develop and effect others? Any further trouble brings great joy to the devil as it spreads to others and causes damage in their lives too. Jesus has cures freely available if you will only come to Him and seek His help. Let His love develop in your heart and give Him the glory in all you do and say.

PRAYER – Father, please help me to deal with anything in my life that is not faithful and true. Give me the desire to share Your love and purposes with all my contacts.

JANUARY 14th

Hebrews 10v35-38   Hebrews 12v1-3   James 1v2-4

Watching horses and riders competing in a cross-country race soon reveals the condition of each rider and horse. They all start together, then some begin to slow down, others falter at the jumps while others race ahead confident of a place in the finals.

Do you find life is like a race? Some folks soon slow down as they journey through the Christian way. Others falter when they come to complicated obstacles, while others go sailing through life and seem to cope with problems as if they did not exist. The secret is for you to have a complete trust in the Lord, confident that He will keep you going and that the problems are there for a purpose. Confident too, with sincere determination and trust, that you will reach a place in the finals.

PRAYER – Father, please help me to persevere. It is so easy to be distracted in my 'race' through life, but as I run with Jesus, I know He will help me to take a place in the finish.

JANUARY 15th

Deuteronomy 30v19-20   Psalm 37v3-4   John 12v35-36

Electricity comes from a generator and is directed to the various light sources and pieces of equipment that it supplies. The end is lightness in the darkness and activity through the equipment.

As you study the Word of God, do you rely on Him for your daily supply of energy and light? As you put your life into the hands of the Lord things will begin to happen. You will have light and joy in your life and you will want to praise God for His love and goodness. You will be more enthusiastic for the tasks He sets before you and you will long to share His love and peace with folks who cross your path. You must however, be faithful and obedient and never doubt God's guidance and wisdom on all you think and do.

PRAYER – Father, sometimes I look ahead and wonder. Then I realise that You are speaking and I stop to listen to Your 'still small voice' and I trust You and thank You for attracting my attention.

JANUARY 16th

Psalm 119v33-35   Romans 12v3-8   1Peter 4v7-11

Dogs have a very acute sense of smell. In the beginning they pick up the scent of what they are tracking down, then, with nose to the ground, they concentrate all the way to the target.

God has called each one of us to follow the Christian way with a particular gift. Do you follow any particular trail? We do not all have the same gifts, but having sought out the scent of years, concentrate in using your particular gift for His glory. Do not be put off by those who try to dissuade you. Moses was given the gift of leadership and he led the Children of Israel through the desert as God had asked him to do. He did not doubt; he obeyed. So must you, then together we can go forward rejoicing in what the Lord can do with our meagre contributions along the way.

PRAYER – Father, thank you for the gift You have given me. Help me to use it for Your glory and not try to put obstacles in the way, or be distracted.

JANUARY 17th

Acts 9v31   1Thessalonians 2v10-12   Hebrews 10v19-25

The winter will soon pass, then buds will begin to appear on the trees and bushes. Bulbs lying dormant will begin to wake and it won't be long before little green shoots will peep through the soil.

Your Christian life will lie dormant unless something happens to wake it up. Do you feel dormant or are you considering the future? To 'awake out of sleep' you will need encouragement. Turn to God and His Word; there you will find all the encouragement you need. You will stir with enthusiasm and long to serve the Lord in whatever way He guides you to do so.

PRAYER – Father, I long to play my part in Your tapestry of life. I thank you that I can turn to You, and I pray that I will always be ready to take action as soon as You encourage me to do so.

JANUARY 18th

Joshua 1v7-9   Psalm 27v3-6   John 20v30-31

When we write letters we start with the usual formalities. Our address, the date and name of the person to whom we are writing. Then we follow on with what we have to say, greetings, thank you, sympathy or just news. We look forward to hearing back from them.

In prayer you are speaking to God. You cannot see Him but you know that He will hear and receive your prayer and will answer it in due course. When you write or read about Jesus, do you think about Him and picture Him in your mind? Remember to head your prayer correctly, sharing your joys and sorrows. Be interested in what God is doing and has done through Jesus when He was down here on earth and now does through His Spirit. Keep a picture of Jesus in your mind and look forward to His return in due course, or the time when you will meet Him face to face.

PRAYER – Father, I am so thankful that You are always ready to hear my prayer. You do not always answer as I expect, but I know that it is always for the best in the long run.

JANUARY 19th

Psalm 18v30   Proverbs 22v19   Hebrews 10v35

To get to a certain destination we need to use some kind of transport. We put complete trust in the driver of the car, train or bus, assuming that he knows the way. In putting your trust in him, you will eventually reach your destination.

When you started into the Christian pilgrimage did you trust the 'Driver'? You can be certain that He knew what He was doing and where He was going. Jesus is your 'Driver' along the Christian way and you need to have complete confidence in Him. He will take care of you and guide your life in the way He directs it, making sure not to go along the wrong road. It is just for you to 'stay on board' and know that you will arrive safely at your destination.

PRAYER – Father, Thank you that I can always trust Jesus to take me safely to my destination. May I never be tempted to doubt.

JANUARY 20th

2Corinthians 8v17   2Corinthians 9v2   Philippians 4v13

Have you watched an ant following a trail through the woods? It moves with determination along the trail set before it, confident that it will eventually reach the end of the journey, despite the woodland undergrowth that tends to disrupt the journey en route.

There will be barriers along the way you go, but do not be distracted. Are you determined to follow the Christian way despite disruptions on the way? God knows about these barriers, in fact He often causes them to test and strengthen your faith. Remember how Job was constantly confronted by barriers, but he kept going and never let his trust in God falter. Eventually, he received his reward in abundance because he had faith in God. You must have the same attitude too.

PRAYER – Father, I do not understand the problems that confront me but I know You understand and have allowed them to happen for a good reason.

JANUARY 21st

1Corinthians 12v4   Colossians 1v5-6   2Timothy 2v15

When a book is written, the author will plan it all out in some kind of order before he begins to write. The story must have substance and style and be applicable to the readers. This must all take place at the very beginning.

We are all made differently and we all have special gifting. Do you have a well thought out plan for your life? Do you stop to consider what gifts you have or perhaps what kind of lifestyle your particular character will match? What about the people with whom you come into contact day by day; family, work mates etc. In seeking to proclaim the Good News of the Gospel, we all have different methods of presentation. Spend time in the Word of God as Jesus guides you in the right direction and gives you the wisdom to do and say the right things.

PRAYER – Father, I am keen to share my experiences of what Jesus and the Scriptures mean to me. Please help me to follow the guide lines of my Lord and Master, Jesus Christ Who will guide me in the right presentation.

JANUARY 22nd

Romans 5v17   1Peter 2v2   1Peter 4v11

It will soon be time for baby animals to make their spring appearance. Have you watched nature at work as newly born animals soon struggle to stand and then seek immediate nourishment from their mothers? Wonderful, and all done by instinct!

As you are born into a new life to be spent with our Lord and Saviour, Jesus Christ, how do you react? As the truth dawns through the guidance of the Holy Spirit, you will immediately want to 'get going'. Then your first requirement must be to turn to the Word of God. Here you will find strength and spiritual nourishment. Do not neglect this important step which will guide you through the way ahead. Always follow the Lord and do not leave His side. If you are tempted to wander remember, danger lurks ahead and you may regret such steps.

PRAYER – Father, as I start out on the way ahead, please help me to keep close to the wonderful source of supply that encourages me to follow Jesus. How I praise You for Your wonderful provision.

JANUARY 23rd

Psalm 32v8   Romans 15v5-6   Colossians 4v7-9

The postage rate seems to be continually rising, but without stamps we cannot send a letter. Without sending a letter we are unable to keep up friendships and contacts unless we are equipped with modern technology.

Are you able to keep in touch with God by spending more time with Jesus? Do you set time aside each day to read a particular message in Scripture? Throughout Scripture you will find records of Biblical history. These records were all written by men inspired by the Spirit of God. As you read them, consider that the message or letter you read was written for your benefit; a word from the Lord to guide you on your way. Act upon it and you will be conscious of a real link with the Lord. Be obedient, follow His guiding and you will never regret it.

PRAYER – Father, thank you for Your Word and for all those men who, inspired by You, were able to convey messages to alert and encourage me day by day.

JANUARY 24th

Psalm 27v14   Matthew 24v37   Revelation 22v7-13

Most of us enjoy going to the theatre or other form of entertainment from time to time. We take our seats and wait for the start of the show. We are full of expectation and as the lights dim and the curtains draw back, we feel an sense of excitement and enthusiasm. Ah! It has started!

Do you ever think about the return of Jesus to planet earth in this way? Surely this is an occasion to get excited about. For the time being you are, as it were, taking your seat and waiting in anticipation. But in this case you need to keep 'serving the Lord' knowing that He is coming but anxious to keep on doing the tasks He has given you to do, and to alert those with whom you are in contact. At the same time, you will be ready and wait anxiously and full of excitement for that glorious day.

PRAYER – Father, it is so wonderful to know that Jesus, Your beloved Son, is coming back to planet earth to reign in glory and majesty. Help me to be ready and to alert others who have doubts.

JANUARY 25th

Matthew 7v24-27   Luke 14v28-30   1Corinthians 3v10-15

Foundations are important. They are the beginning of something that needs to be secure. A house would not last long unless it was built on a firm foundation.

The foundation of your Christian life is important. Have you spent time with God to seek out His plan and purpose for your life? Through His Word you will find guidance, then as you build on your foundation you will rejoice in the way God will lead you on. He sent Jesus to show us the way, and you need to spend time in His presence, building up your ministry with Him. You will be so thankful and happy that you spent time preparing a good foundation.

PRAYER – Father, as I put my trust in You, help me to build on Your truth and faithfulness. Thank you that Jesus will give me all the help I need to develop, providing I have faith to believe.

JANUARY 26th

1Corinthians 3v5-9   Colossians 1v10-12   2Peter 3v18

When we see the sun shining on a rich crop of corn, swaying in a gentle breeze, we admire the beauty of the scene. But we realise too, that some months earlier, that same land was bear and the now flourishing crop was just a sack of seed, faithfully planted by the farmer.

Have you ever wondered how Christians become so mature? When you are at some big Christian rally perhaps, you are conscious of keen enthusiasm with outstanding singing and preaching, full of the joy of the Lord. In the beginning God had to prepare these folks so that they could develop. In the same way He wants to help you to develop in all you do for Him, so that you too, can bring joy to Him with enthusiasm, that will bring blessings to others too.

PRAYER – Father, thank you for the ability I have to grow and develop and rejoice in You. I realise that this is because of the time and patience You have spent, enabling me to give pleasure to others in my witness and love for You.

JANUARY 27th

       Psalm 119v166-168   Luke 9v23-26   John 12v26

There are times when we suddenly mislay something and cannot think where it is. We look in places where we think it might be but eventually find it in the most unlikely place.

The Christian life can be very like this. Do you sometimes think of something you should be doing but you are conscious that God is directing you to something else? You suddenly mislay the task of witness you thought was your duty to perform. God has other plans; do not ignore them. Seek His guidance, go where He leads and you will be so glad you did so. People are waiting for you and the Lord knows where He wants you to be.

PRAYER – Father, What a good thing it is that You keep a track on me. Please guide me in the right direction and help me to be obedient in my response.

JANUARY 28th

       Isaiah 49v1-2   Matthew 8v1-2   Hebrews 10v19-25

We like to see our homes cared for and a spot of polish on the furniture makes all the difference. The more we polish the brighter is the outcome and the scent of the polish makes everything so fresh.

It will be necessary for you to polish up your Christian life from time to time. Do you ever think of polishing up your thoughts about God and His plans for you? You may need to rub hard to remove any stains, then bring up a shine so that your life radiates the love of God. This will probably mean a re-examination of your lifestyle to clear out the bits that are spoiling your Christian witness. In so doing, you will develop and grow in your faith and ministry for the Lord.

PRAYER – Father, help me to shine for You and be able to radiate Your love to the contacts I have each day. Thank you for Jesus and His Spirit that makes it all possible.

JANUARY 29th

Matthew 17v20-21   Mark 10v27   Hebrews 11v6

When you watch a squirrel chasing up a tree, one marvels at the way he seems to cling to the bark and run so fast at the same time. Then he leaps from one tree to another landing safely on a flimsy branch. Quite amazing!

Are you prepared to keep moving in this way in your daily walk with the Lord? As you travel along the Christian way so often the route is uphill. You need to climb on, and this can only be done by keeping close to your Lord and Master, Jesus Christ, in prayer communication and Bible study all the way. If you are prepared to do that, you will be confronted with all He wants you to do in your life. This may well mean leaping into the unknown; a task you envisage as impossible, but if that's what He wants you to do, He will give you the ability to do it.

PRAYER – Father, as I sometimes face an impossible situation, give me the courage and determination to keep going, knowing that Jesus will guide me all the way.

JANUARY 30th

Matthew 3v3   Ephesians 3v9-13   1Peter 1v13-16

Furniture comes from trees which have to be selected and felled, then cut and shaped according to the requirements of a particular item of furniture for which it is intended.

God has selected you for a particular task but before you can do that task you need to be prepared. Are you conscious of God's hand directing you? Consider it a privilege to be chosen, and seek to follow where He leads. Accept correction and sometimes difficult circumstances, as part of the preparation programme that God thinks is necessary in His plan for your life. The end result should reveal a life of loveliness fit for the Lord's service wherever He desires to use you.

PRAYER – Father, I am not always prepared to follow the way You want me to go. Please make me determined to stand up to Satan's subtle ways and to blend in with Your desires for my life.

JANUARY 31st

Psalm 119v105   1Corinthians 6v19-20   1Peter 2v2-3

To keep alive, men and all creatures need a constant supply of food and water to sustain the living body. From the very start, a baby needs to take nourishment in the form of milk. It is essential that we take care of our bodies.

Your Christian life needs to be constantly fed and nurtured if you are to grow and develop in your faith and your daily witness for God. Do you always remember to spend time with God in your daily routine? You need to start with the milk of the Word, then progress and develop as you become stronger. Remember how essential this is and what a privilege to be able to turn to Him whatever the situation, whether happy or difficult. Remember too, that your body is a temple of the Holy Spirit. We are all responsible to take care of our bodies.

PRAYER – Father, I long to spend time in Your presence and to listen to You as I read the Scriptures. Thank you for the privilege of always being in Your care.

FEBRUARY

FEBRUARY 1st

Psalm 84v11-12   Daniel 12v3   Acts 26v13

What a difference the sun makes in life. Everything looks so bright and fresh and this makes us feel so good. When the sun stops shining, everything looks dull and dreary, and we tend not to feel so good.

Is Jesus the light in your life? If so, it will be like the brightness of the sun and you will feel able to cope with whatever situation confronts you each day. Reading through the Scriptures, time and again you will notice the transformation of many lives, confirming the fact that His light gives a radiance like nothing else. Those concerned are conscious of an inner strength and joy not known before. Be sure you are one of His followers too.

PRAYER – Father, please help me to be joyful in Your love and to follow the way You lead. Thank you that I know that Jesus will radiate through me when I put my trust in Him.

FEBRUARY 2nd

Matthew 22v1-10   Matthew 25v1-13   Revelation 19v6-9

When there is a wedding in the family everyone begins to look forward to the event. As the time draws near excitement begins to increase. The flowers arrive, the bride is dressed. All is ready; the car arrives, then to the church. The moment has come at last.

In a similar way, as a Christian family, we should begin to look forward to that promised day when Jesus will return to planet earth to meet His bride, the church. Do you ever get excited about this event? You need to carry on as usual, but at the same time, be ready. Prepare all that is necessary and take each step one at a time. The time and day will be made clear in due course. Just keep your eyes upon the Bridegroom and know that He will surely come.

PRAYER – Father, what an exciting event is going to take place when you decide the time for 'the wedding of the Lamb.' Help me to be ready to join in the excitement. I praise You for this wonderful occasion.

FEBRUARY 3rd

Job 5v17-22   Proverbs 10v17   Romans 8v28

There are times when we find it difficult to agree with someone and we tend to get frustrated. Then that person suddenly changes and before you know it, he or she decides that your idea was better after all. How pleased you are and so thankful that you did not condemn them.

Sometimes the Lord corrects you in a way that troubles you and causes you to question why certain things are happening as they are. Do you have occasions like this? Whatever the problem is, you need to go through it believing that God has a purpose in allowing it to happen. He is testing and training you. In due course He will reveal the reason and you will be amazed at the outcome which will cause you to be so full of praise for the Lord who in His wisdom allowed you to experience His love.

PRAYER – Father, why did I doubt You? I ask Your forgiveness and pray that I will always have faith to know that You know what is best for me anyway.

FEBRUARY 4th

Psalm 5v11   Psalm 37v3-4   1Timothy 6v17

Have you ever been at sea and passed through a school of dolphins? Have you seen how they leap out of the water? It is exciting to watch just where they are going to pop up next as they seem to be so joyful in their activities.

When you are doing something that you enjoy doing, do you have a feeling of satisfaction? Now you will notice a sense of joy in your life when you are serving the Lord in the place of God's appointment for you. There may be difficult patches in this particular task or ministry, but the Lord will give you a wonderful consciousness of His presence which will give you a sense of joy in your heart to overcome the difficulties.

PRAYER – Father, there are lots of things that make me happy, but I know that the only real joy in my heart can only be when I am doing the thing that You have chosen for me to do. I love You, Lord.

FEBRUARY 5th

Psalm 68v3   Psalm 118v24   Philippians 4v4-7

Walking along the seaside promenade in the summer, what happy scenes we see. The gentle lapping of the waves on the sea shore, the children building sand castles, excited people splashing in the water, ice creams, deck chairs, playful dogs. Everyone is so happy.

Have you been to a Christian Crusade at some time? Listen to the joyful singing and the uplifting prayers, to say nothing of the soul stirring message. Does this not stimulate your faith in God? You must try to extend this stimulation into your every day life. Jesus never told you to be sad, but He does understand your feelings. So as you put your trust in Him, you will find your thoughts will turn to so much that can bring real joy to your life. Try it.

PRAYER – Father, I really do want to feel the joy that You give, in my heart and I want to share it with my contacts today. Keep me trusting You in the knowledge that You can make this possible.

FEBRUARY 6th

Psalm 40v16   Matthew 6v28-34   Matthew 28v18-20

At this time of the year we begin to watch the spring flowers developing and it is a joy to see them grow. This month the snowdrops will be waving their pretty heads in the breeze.

Life is full of exciting experiences and one of the most enjoyable times is when we see people coming to know and love Jesus. The transformation in their lives is a thrill to behold. You will know this surely. How do you react? Be present at an evangelistic rally, for example, and be conscious of the 'thrill in the air' as men, women and children make the greatest decision of their lives. We all have a certain responsibility to make Jesus known, and to share in the joy resulting from that special relationship.

PRAYER – Father, thank you for sending Jesus to live and die that I might live. May my life show forth His love in all I do and say.

FEBRUARY 7th

Proverbs 27v8   Jeremiah 24v7   Luke 15v11-31

When part of our family has been away for a while, we miss them. Then when they return, we are so pleased to see them and tend to celebrate their homecoming.

Remember the prodigal son. He went away from home, spent his life recklessly, then realised that home was best. Have you at some time 'gone away from home;' have you gone away from Jesus? If you have strayed from the way, come back. The Father is waiting to welcome you home. As you come back, there will be much rejoicing and celebrating as love flows freely.

PRAYER – Father, help me not to wander away from You, but if I do stray, give me the desire to return, and to experience the love You give me in so doing.

FEBRUARY 8th

Psalm 4v6-8   Psalm 139v12   2Corinthians 4v6

Have you ever been lost on a woodland walk? It can be a bit scary, especially if it is beginning to get dark. Then you see a gap of light and you go for it! You come out of the woods and rejoice that the path leads you out of your anxieties.

When you are confronted with a host of problems in your Christian life, do you become confused and sometimes fearful? You must look for the light of God's love and then go in that direction. You will then find that the path before you will lead straight to that light and you will have cause to rejoice and be thankful. The host of difficulties through which you have just passed will not seem so terrible after all.

PRAYER – Father, please help me to unravel myself from the problems that surround me, as I look ahead to Your wonderful light.

FEBRUARY 9th

Psalm 37v5   Romans 9v17   2Timothy 1v9

A butterfly starts life in a cocoon. As it slowly breaks out of the cocoon, one is tempted to help, but this would be destructive. It must tackle this alone. Suddenly it will emerge and fly away, happy and free to bring joy to us all.

How do you break out of your normal routine to be free to serve the Lord? It is not always easy but there is a needy world out there and God needs each one of us, as His children, to witness for Him. He positions us all in different places and we all have different gifts. Until you break out of your routine and commit your life to Jesus, you will never be able to fulfil the purpose for which He intended you. When you respond, such joy will fill your heart.

PRAYER – Father, I am so content and comfortable in my routine programme through life. Please give me the desire to draw closer to You and to seek Your will for my life.

FEBRUARY 10th

Proverbs 25v25   Luke 1v39-45   John 15v11

Exam results bring one of two reactions. Either there is disappointment because of failure, or there is excitement because of success. It can make all the difference to ones feelings.

Search through Scripture and notice the reactions experienced in the Old Testament by prophets or by day to day people. Do you experience these reactions in your day to day experiences? Remember the excitement Elizabeth showed when Mary told her about her pregnancy. When you have thrilling news from a friend, you will reveal some way to show how pleased you are. It is important that we encourage one another in this way and so give praise to our Lord.

PRAYER – Father, I get excited when I consider how You give me the joy of being happy. Help me to share these moments with others and so give You glory.

FEBRUARY 11th

Psalm 42v1-2   John 8v32   2Timothy 4v1-2

There are so many people in the world that are starving and homeless. Various agencies do what they can to help, but the needs are many and great. What joy it is for the people when they receive the help of food, water and shelter.

The world is full of people hungry and thirsty for the Word of God. What part can you play in helping these folk? We all need to be involved in one way or another. As a Christian, committed to the task of making God known and introducing folk to Jesus, never give up. If people turn away, you have done your duty in sharing what you know to be true. Your desire is that they too, should know the truth and be set free, to share the joy of the Lord too .

PRAYER - Father, I do try, but so often people just don't want to know. Give me a greater desire to share Your love, joy and peace amongst so many needy people.

FEBRUARY 12th

Ezekiel 34v12   Luke 15v8-10   Philippians 3v7-9

What an anxious time it is if your wallet goes missing. You do not remember when you last saw it or where you put it. Suddenly you find it in a most unexpected place. What   excitement! The lost is found.

Have you ever been confronted with a situation that has arisen, causing you to go away from the Lord for any reason? Have you ever thought how God has felt when this happens? Remember the story of Jacob and Joseph. The sadness in Jacob's heart when Joseph was reported dead. Then the glorious joy he had when it was proved that Joseph was alive. Never cease to praise the Lord when He is able to find you restored and back in a loving relationship.

PRAYER – Father, thank you for Your care and concern. Forgive me for my foolish ways and accept me back into your family. What joy now fills my heart.

FEBRUARY 13th

Psalm 91v14-16   Isaiah 63v9   Hebrews 12v2

How lovely it is to watch soft snowflakes gently falling on to the trees and bushes, glistening in the winter sunshine. We know that snow can cause many problems, but we can still admire the beauty of such a scene.

As the sunshine of God's love reveals such beauty as it alights upon us, so problems tend to disturb the depth of that love. Are you conscious of God's love as you move from day to day? Look in Scripture and discover the many times His love has descended to bring beauty, relief and joy to so many of the Bible characters, enabling them to rejoice and praise the God and Father of us all. Trust Him and keep your eyes upon Jesus.

PRAYER – Father, I rejoice as I see Your love descending and realise how beautiful it is. Thank you for giving me so much pleasure to overcome the unhappy moments in life.

FEBRUARY 14th

John 14v1-3   2Corinthians 5v1-10   1Peter 5v7

Holidays are great but somehow it is lovely to get home again. Back to familiar surroundings and regular routine. A feeling of happiness; coming home.

Christians are on the way Home; something to look forward to. Do you have a sense of happiness as you enjoy all the experiences of this life? Some occasions will not be enjoyable perhaps, but do not be anxious. Jesus, in His final weeks suffered so much, but He did not give in. He spent His life here on earth, doing His Father's will. He knew where He was going and enjoyed the life He had spent helping folks and sharing the love of His Father. You must follow in His footsteps. Love your neighbour and do good wherever you are as you make your way Home.

PRAYER – Father, I am looking forward to coming Home. Please help me to find the way and to witness faithfully for You en route. I will rejoice in the reunion there will be one day.

FEBRUARY 15th

John 3v16   Romans 6v23   James 1v17

It is always such a happy time as we open gifts on birthdays or other celebrations. Either by letter or word, we will want to thank the person who gave us so much pleasure.

God gave you the most precious gift you will ever receive when He gave His Son to deal with your past sins. In obedience to His Father, Jesus gave His life for you. How do you respond to such a gift? It should cause you to want to rejoice, thanking and praising God for His love. For His goodness and consideration give Him your all and seek to follow the example of Jesus. Remember your family and friends too, giving to them, in whatever way is applicable.

PRAYER – Father, I will never be able to thank you enough for all You have given to me through Your Son, Jesus Christ. I praise You, my Father, for caring so much for me.

FEBRUARY 16th

Matthew 24v44   Matthew 25v1-13   Luke 12v35-37

Watch the crowds at a football match. All of a sudden a goal is scored and the crowds seem to go mad with their yells and shouts of excitement and praise for the winning team.

Are you beginning to get ready for Jesus' return? The day will come but no one knows when. You need to be in a state of anticipation as you wait in expectation. Be prepared to rejoice and sing in sheer celebration of the occasion. As you wait, enthuse others too, so that they can also prepare for that great day.

PRAYER – Father, I look forward to the time when I will meet Jesus. It may be when He calls me Home or it may be when He comes back Himself once again to planet earth. Whatever, I want to be ready.

FEBRUARY 17th

Psalm 5v3   Matthew 6v6   Philippians 4v6-7

When you suddenly hear from someone whom you have not heard from for a long time, how exciting it is to catch up on news.

This is how it is with God. He has not heard from you for a long time. Have you spoken to Him recently? When you do, He will be so thrilled and despite your neglect, He will not hold any ill feelings but will welcome you gladly. He will be ready to hear all about what you have done with your life. Give Him a full report and listen to His news too. Then go on your way rejoicing. He is always more ready to give than we are to receive.

PRAYER – Father, I am so glad I 'got in touch' with You again. Forgive me that I have neglected you for so long. I am so happy to be in such close contact with You.

FEBRUARY 18th

Isaiah 59v1-2   1John 1v8-9   1John 2v1-2

Sometimes baby animals get separated from their mothers. Both become very stressed and search for one another. Someone realises the situation and unites them together again. What rejoicing results from the reunion.

Are you ever conscious of being separated from God? Somehow He does not seem to be near you any more. Listen, Jesus is always ready to bring you back to the Father, so let Him take your life and bring you safely back, but you need to be willing. Then when the union is complete, you will be filled with the desire to worship your God and Father, with praise and adoration.

PRAYER – Father, thank you that Jesus has brought me back into Your family. I worship and praise You.

FEBRUARY 19th

Isaiah 63v9   Philippians 4v6   James 1v2-4

Training a child can be very frustrating. You spend time, try to be kind, but often have to 'lay down the law.' But all the time you love him/her and want the best. The end result can be very rewarding.

We are all God's children and He loves us. He wants the best for you, but do you always respond as you should? Refer to the Scriptures and read about the Children of Israel and His loving care for them when they left Egypt. They had to experience many hardships as they travelled through the wilderness. Then they complained, but God still loved them and provided for them in every way. Do not get frustrated when things go wrong. God still loves you; He is disciplining you for your good. Rejoice and be glad and give Him the glory.

PRAYER – Father, I do praise You for Your Fatherly love. Forgive me for the times I get cross. I really do thank you in every situation.

FEBRUARY 20th

Matthew 4v23-24   Matthew 9v36-38   James 2v14-18

There are so many refugee situations in the world today; so many unhappy people, homeless and hungry. Charity services do what they can to bring joy and relief to those who suffer so much.

Jesus spent so much of His time on earth helping people, healing the sick and bringing peace and happiness to so many. We are disciples of Jesus. Do you try to follow His example? There are so many folk with whom we come into contact day by day. You need to help where you can, showing the love and compassion of Jesus in all you do and say. Pass on a word of comfort or encouragement and show them that you care. In order to be equipped with compassion you need to keep in close contact with the Lord every moment.

PRAYER – Father, I need Your guiding hand to make me what I need to be as I seek to follow Jesus and help the folk with whom I come into contact day by day.

FEBRUARY 21st

Daniel 12v3   Matthew 3v11   Hebrews 1v7

A fire starts with a spark, then the warmth of the initial spark spreads and gradually a fire develops and spreads, bringing warmth and cheerful comfort as it burns.

The Christian life is like a fire in your life. Have you received the 'spark' yet? As your experience develops, you can become so much more help to so many people as you share the love of Jesus in all that you do. But you must have the 'spark' to help you share the fire of God and this means drawing close to the only One who can enable you to grow and shine wherever He sends you in this needy world.

PRAYER – Father, kindle the flame in my heart to show forth Your love amongst the contacts I have today.

FEBRUARY 22nd

Psalm 36v9   Isaiah 60v20   2Peter 1v19

Travelling through a long tunnel seems an impossible journey. Then all of a sudden a light is visible at the end of the tunnel. The darkness is nearly over and a sense of release and thankfulness is felt.

When you are going through a rough patch in your life, how do you feel? Do you feel a sense of despondency? Take heart, look up, because there is an end to this feeling and in due course you will see a light ahead which will encourage you and give you a sense of God's presence that will make you feel enthusiastic once more. Every act of God in your life is designed to increase your dependence on Him.

PRAYER – Father, so often the way seems dark and difficult. I am so thankful that there is a light at the end of my present experience.

FEBRUARY 23rd

Proverbs 3v5   John 14v27   Hebrews 13v7

There are occasions when we have a sleepless night. We toss and turn and so many thoughts go through our head. Then we tend to get busy planning tomorrows schedule. Is this familiar?

Do you sometimes have difficulty in praying? Even reading the Scriptures is a problem. You are all upset and don't know what to do. It is good to share your feelings with a close friend or counsellor who can at least guide you in the right direction. But better than anything else, come to Jesus, rest in His love and think about lovely things, beautiful scenes or special occasions. Forget about the problems of yesterday or possible happenings of tomorrow. Just concentrate on today and relax. You will be amazed how soon you will be singing again.

PRAYER – Father, I thank you for loving and understanding friends, but above all I thank You for your peace. I want to praise You for all You mean to me.

FEBRUARY 24th

Psalm 19v12-14   Matthew 8v1-3   2Corinthians 6v14 to 7v1

This time of the year we begin to realise that winter will soon be past and we need to think about spring cleaning. This will involve extra work and often the discovery of dust and dirt behind the furniture etc. But what a lovely feeling when everything is clean again.

Do you ever have a spiritual spring clean? It is necessary to get things sorted and cleaned up from time to time. Sometimes you will not find it easy to do, and you may discover hidden 'dirt' you did not realise was there. Jesus wants you to have a 'clean bill of health.' Speak to Him, search the Scriptures and listen to His instructions. Do not falter but keep your house in order. It will bring you such a feeling of joy and pleasure when everything is looking good.

PRAYER – Father, I want to present my life clean and clear of obstructions. I need Your help in order to do this properly.

FEBRUARY 25th

Psalm 32v8   Psalm 73v21-26   Romans 12v1-2

When we are learning something new, it is easy to make a mistake. We don't mean to and we try our best to work out what has gone wrong. When we discover the right way we are very pleased.

There are times when we all make mistakes in our decisions. Do you hear what God is saying but consider the choice you have made is the best? You may not fancy His choice but it is necessary for you to obey. God does not waste words, and calling you His way has a purpose. Remember, you are still in training and often this will mean tackling a rough patch. This must be in order to improve His future plans for you. Do not hesitate, but praise Him for His guidance and wisdom. You will not be disappointed.

PRAYER – Father, my nature often calls me to reject Your desire for me to follow the way You lead. Please help me to be more 'in tune' with You, Lord.

FEBRUARY 26th

Psalm 46v1-2   Matthew 11v10   Hebrews 3v6

Winter has not yet passed and there is still time for snow and ice to disrupt the daily routine and cause travel delays. Eventually, we reach our destination and are so thankful to arrive safely.

Do you come up against delays in your daily routine? There are always going to be delays and disruptions on the Christian pathway, but this is all part of life and you need to face up to the fact that you have to keep going. Maybe you can help someone at this time, who is also caught up in trouble. We are encouraged to help one another. The 'snow' may blot out the road and the 'ice' cause you to slip. You have Jesus to hold your hand however difficult the way may be. When you finally get to your destination, you will have so much for which to be thankful.

PRAYER – Father, Your way is not easy but I will persevere because Jesus will always help me over the problems. I thank you; I am so grateful that You send Him to my rescue.

FEBRUARY 27th

Isaiah 30v15&18   Matthew 9v18-26   John 15v11-12

Much of the routine shopping today is done in huge supermarkets. Gone are the days of the small, friendly village shops where time could be spent exchanging village news and generally enjoying friendly fellowship.

It is so important to have time for people. Everyone is in a hurry today with no time to consider others in a relaxed, happy atmosphere. Do you enjoy rushing through life or do you stop to remember your friends and contacts, and reserve part of your time to consider their needs or to cheer and encourage them where necessary? As Christian men and women this is our responsibility. Jesus was never in a hurry; He always had time and concern for everyone. You should follow His example and share His love too.

PRAYER – Father, may the love of Jesus radiate through my life and bring joy to those with whom I have contact day by day. Please forgive me when I rush, Lord. Please calm me down.

FEBRUARY 28th

Matthew 5v14-16   1John 1v3-4   1John 5v4-5

When monkeys get together in the tropical treetops they love to leap from branch to branch, chattering and playing together. Generally they have such fun, and are so exciting to watch.

Our Christian lives should be lives of excitement. What do you spend time enjoying most? Fellowship with Christian friends brings so much encouragement. You have a responsibility to do this and consider it a privilege to share your faith. God does not want you to hibernate but to go forward. When you tend to feel discouraged if someone does not respond amicably, turn to the Lord and seek His encouragement. Remember, He delights to do His Father's will and He wants you to delight in your witness too.

PRAYER – Father, I need to feel the presence of Your love in my heart, so that I may be a help and encouragement in my service for You.

FEBRUARY 29th

Psalm 73v23-24   John 16v13   Hebrews 12v1-3

When we travel on the roads, we are confronted by a host of road signs indicating where and where not we go or what or what not we can do. If these rules are ignored, accidents will occur.

The Christian life is full of signs directing us as we go. Do you always obey the instructions that confront you? When you see a sign telling you not to follow a certain route, you must keep on until you find the right way. Jesus is always near you and ready to protect you from making mistakes. Sometimes you may want to rest for a while. Make sure you stop in the allocated area, and so spend time of refreshment in God's presence before you carry on.

PRAYER – Father, it is so easy to make mistakes, to take the wrong road or to stop in the wrong place. Please protect me along the way. Thank you that Jesus is always with me to guide me as I seek to obey Your Word.

MARCH

MARCH 1st

Romans 5v8   1Timothy 6v17b   Hebrews 12v2

Planet earth is full of so many lovely things for us to enjoy but man has introduced so much that spoils the beauty of God's creation.

Christmas is past and now we begin to look forward to Easter and springtime. We are almost into the time of Lent. How do you approach this time? Many thoughts will turn your eyes towards Jesus, God's precious Son, sent to earth to rescue us from all the sins penetrating into God's world. Come into the very presence of Jesus and commit your life afresh to Him as the Easter season approaches. Remember all that He did for you in obedience to His Father.

PRAYER – Father, I have so much to remember as I recommit my life to Jesus and try to follow the way He leads me through the beauty of Your creation here on earth.

MARCH 2nd

John 14v6   Romans 10v14-15   Hebrews 7v24-25

Animals can be very unkind to one another and often do not appreciate any help that is offered. They always know best!

Today there are many people who do not seem to recognise the love of Jesus. They may believe in God, but that is as far as it gets. Do you try to encourage people? You need to show forth God's love in practical ways and be filled with enthusiasm, to introduce them to the One who can enter into their lives and give them assurance of Eternal Life.

PRAYER – Father, lead me to the people who will listen to You, as I seek to guide them into a true relationship with Jesus.

MARCH 3rd

Deuteronomy 31v8   Isaiah 12v2   Matthew 28v20

When we are confronted by a mass of heavy traffic, driving on a busy motorway, we can feel somewhat scary. The huge lorries seem to swamp us and they tend to block direction signs. The situation is not pleasant.

Life can be scary. Do you sometimes stop and wonder how you are going to cope? God tells you not to be afraid. He promises to go ahead of you and however difficult the problem, He will always be with you. The Scripture does not lie and you will read specifically that God will never forsake you. If you believe what you read, how can you doubt or have fear?

PRAYER – Father, it seems natural to be fearful but I do believe what You tell me about Your constant care and guidance. Please help me to increase my trust in You.

MARCH 4th

John 3v16   2Corinthians 5v1   Hebrews 5v8-9

Archaeologists are discovering new finds every week. Structures and remains dating back thousands of years. It would appear that these finds will go on for ever.

Are you looking forward to an eternal future? We are told that God's free gift of His Son, Jesus, will enable all of us to receive Eternal Life, but there is a condition. You need to recognise that sin and death came into the world because we are all related to Adam, where the sinful race of man began. Wherever there is sin, death results. If you have accepted Jesus into your life, you are taking the way to everlasting life through trusting Him. God wants to save the world and you will want to be part of this glorious truth.

PRAYER – Father, I am so happy to know that You call me to be part of a wonderful future. Help me to be willing to accept your perfect gift, Jesus, to guide me all the way Home.

MARCH 5th

Habakkuk 3v17   Matthew 7v17-20   John 15v1-8

As spring approaches nature wakes up. The trees and bushes begin to bud. The fruit tree buds will eventually develop to produce fruit. But if the branch is broken it will not be possible for fruit to form.

Jesus is the main centre of the Vine and we are the branches. Do you produce fruit in your Christian life? Do not let your life break away from Jesus. Follow Him always and give Him full control. As He does so, the Holy Spirit enables your life to be filled with love for Him and a desire to serve God wherever He sends you. Trust and obey, there is no other way. Strong in the Lord and in the power of His might.

PRAYER – Father, I want my life to be a strong branch, never to break away from Your loving care. Help me to be responsible for a good crop of 'fruit.'

MARCH 6th

Psalm 36v7-9   Isaiah 41v10   1Timothy 4v9-10

In the heat of battle there are dangers all around. The guns roar and bullets fly. Fear grips the hearts of those who are involved but they must fight on.

Life is full of dangers. Do you face any problems that cause you to be afraid? Remember, God protects you under the shadow of His wings. You will face situations that will terrify, but if you have a sound faith, you will be aware of a strength that you did not know you had. Just look to Jesus and face up to the problem; it is there for a purpose and whatever the outcome, God knows what He is doing and why He is doing it. Trust Him, your Refuge and your Rock.

PRAYER – Father, accept me as I am with all my doubts and fears. Help me to put my trust in You, confident that You are my place of safety.

MARCH 7th

Psalm 29v2   Psalm 95v6-7   Revelation 15v3b-4

Technical development is always on the increase. Elderly people, on the whole, find it so difficult to understand, yet they are expected to 'slot in' and keep up with all the improvements.

Sometimes churches have serious differences when it comes to worship. How do you get on with modern choruses and 'songs' ? These days the church possibly has to deal with 3 generations at a time and this is not easy. Don't be critical or complain. Try to accept the fact that things do change, and you should try to 'fit in' and at the same time talk to God and ask Him to make you adaptable. Whoever we are and whatever we think, God has the final word. He loves you; love Him too in whatever way you chose to worship.

PRAYER – Father, I love You and ask You to forgive me for thinking everyone should worship You in the same way as I do.

MARCH 8th

Isaiah 30v21   Matthew 7v13-14   John 14v5-6

Paths always lead to somewhere, but sometimes they finish up as 'dead ends.' In a maze, the aim is to chose the right way. There is only one right way.

Life consists of one long road. It is not an easy road; no one ever said it would be. How are you managing to find the way? There are signposts as you go, so that you can be sure you are following the one and only true road which will lead you to the ultimate end; one with Jesus in Eternity. You will come up against problems and choices, but if you take Jesus as your Guide, He will not let you take the wrong turning. He has promised to return to planet Earth; no one knows when, but He will come one day, because we read about it in God's Word. You must always be on the alert and ready. Others must be alerted too.

PRAYER – Father, I want to be ready for Jesus' return. In the meantime, help me to find the right way to go, so that I may be sure that I take no wrong turnings.

MARCH 9th

Psalm 61v1-2   Philippians 4v13   1Peter 5v10-11

At the end of a very busy day with an extra large laundry wash, baking for the weekend etc, tiredness sets in. All of a sudden the larder seems to be empty. You must dash to the shops. There are also many other jobs to do.

Sometimes life seems to be more than you can cope with and you feel overwhelmed. God understands these things. He will give you all the strength you need. If you try to take on more than He expects you to do, there will be a reminder that you stop and consider. Turn to the Word of God and find out the tasks that you really have to do.

PRAYER – Father, please help me to be able to decipher Your way, in my Christian walk. Give me the strength to cope with the tasks of Your choice for me.

MARCH 10th

Matthew 6v25-34   1Peter 3v8-9   1Peter 5v7

We live in a world of hustle and bustle and so often we get caught up in the tangle. There are so many folks homeless, hungry and alone. Many other folks have all they need. Why the difference?

Christians are not immune to the effect that this environment will have on our day to day reactions. Do you become overcome in your daily walk? Trust in the Lord and concentrate on Him. Seek Him in prayer and listen to Him. Jesus has promised never to leave you alone, so if He is always by your side, why do you worry? He knows about the needs of everyone and He expects us to help one another in a way that will bring glory to God. Consider your responsibilities and share what you can.

PRAYER – Father, why is there so much inequality in the world? Forgive us all for neglecting so many unfortunate people. Help me to be concerned.

MARCH 11th

Psalm 121v3-8   Jeremiah 9v23-24   Hebrews 4v15-16

When we take an interest in a certain organisation or project, it is helpful to be kept up to date with developments, otherwise it is difficult to keep track of what is going on.

Do you realise how wonderful it is to know that God is always up to date with your activities and knows all about your future? He is continually in touch with you, even though you may not realise it. Whatever your thoughts, He knows them too. Put your trust in Jesus and He will enable you to keep Satan at bay. Jesus understands your difficulties and temptations and appreciates how human nature tries to get the upper hand. He experienced this too while here on earth. He will teach you how to master weaknesses if you trust Him to do so.

PRAYER – Father, thank you that I can be assured that Jesus understands my human weaknesses. I want to accept His leadership and keep You informed of my activities.

MARCH 12th

Jeremiah 29v11-13   Philippians 1v12-14   1Peter 2v19-21

How tragic it is to see animals wrongly blamed and treated cruelly when they have done nothing to warrant such punishment. So often they never complain or fight back. How sad.

It is easy enough to expect and accept punishment when you do wrong, but not easy when you do what is apparently right, then receive punishment. Do you find this to be so? But why don't you try to praise the Lord when this happens, because you must realise that He will give you the strength, courage and peace to cope with the situation. You may be restless and not understand what is happening but just wait for the Lord to show you what to do. This is all part of training so accept it as such and praise Him for getting you ready to fit into His future plans.

PRAYER – Father, I am so restless. Please help me not to 'fight back' when you punish me. May I be more patient and understanding. Thank you for understanding me.

MARCH 13th

Psalm 22v4   Psalm 65v2-4   Jeremiah 33v2-3

During the Second World War many people tended to become depressed, especially when in the targeted cities, night after night, they had to spend their time in air raid shelters. There was little comfort, constant gunfire and fearful thoughts.

Do you sometimes get depressed and think that God has not heard your cry for help? You need to accept the promise that He understands and will answer you in due course. It is easy to get fearful and expect immediate answers, when you are disturbed by all that is going on around you. Know that God understands and hold on in trust, faith and love. He will not disappoint you.

PRAYER – Father, why do I always get carried away by the situation I am in? I know you understand what is happening and will protect and encourage me when I put my trust in You.

MARCH 14th

Psalm 27v4   2Corinthians 4v6   Hebrews 12v2

Little lambs are beginning to arrive at this time of the year. To pick up a tiny baby and look into its little face, is to look at something so perfect; so beautiful.

To look into the face of Jesus we see perfection and beauty, peace and calm. Do you pray to be like Jesus? You probably find it difficult to even try to be perfect, realising that you have done, said or thought something that is not really Christ like. You need to keep your eyes upon Him day by day, hour by hour and do not let your thoughts wander off to the jobs you have to do. He knows exactly what you are thinking and doing all the time, but He never forgets you.

PRAYER – Father, how wonderful that You even consider me in Your tapestry I thank you for Jesus' love so continually available to me. My desire is to be gentle and loving in my witness to others too. Please help me.

MARCH 15th

Psalm 27v13-14   Psalm 61v1-5   Matthew 27v41-50

As Lent drifts into Easter, people begin to prepare for 'holiday.' Guest centres and attractions start to open and celebrations are planned. Do they really appreciate what Easter is all about?

As we think upon the Easter story, it is quite impossible to imagine the agony Jesus suffered. Do you complain about being tested and tried? Any experience through which you might have passed is nothing in comparison with the great pain Jesus bore. There was a point when He cried out, thinking His Father had forsaken Him, clearly portraying His human self. So when you feel desperate and call out to God, think about this. Jesus rose to such glory afterwards. When you feel things are overpowering, remember that the best is yet to come.

PRAYER – Father, sometimes I do not understand what is happening but I believe You have a reason. As I accept the experience, it will result in Your overpowering love and victory.

MARCH 16th

Psalm 73v23-26   John14v12-16   2Timothy 4v7

As we get older we tend to look back on our past life and notice how different life is today. When we see what is going on now, sometimes we find it difficult to fit in to modern systems.

Life on this earth seems long but to God time does not count and He can call you away at any time. Do you praise God for the life He has given you? Sometimes you will find it difficult to praise when everything seems to be against you. Do not fill yourself with self pity but look up to Jesus and enable Him to fill you with His Spirit, to live in and through you. Consider others as Jesus did and try to help and witness God's love. Reveal a calm life at rest and at peace, despite the confusion of modern living and praise God for opportunities to witness.

PRAYER – Father, life for me is as long as You desire. Help me to accept this fact and be ready when You call. I want to praise You for all you ask me to be and do as I travel along the way.

MARCH 17th

Job 1v6-12   1Corinthians 10v13   1Peter 5v8-11

As plant life is beginning to stir, we need to watch for aphids and other little bugs that delight in attacking young developing buds. We catch them before they damage the whole plant.

Satan is very much alive and is certainly trying to guide you into what he wants for your life. Do you feel the force of this statement? He is, in fact, in competition with Jesus. You need to be aware of this fact when you are praying and plead with God that, in the name of Jesus, Satan will be bound and prevented from any action he has in mind. Sometimes however, God will let Satan have his way to a degree, but only to the extent that I can cope with. God will not allow you to be tempted more than you can manage. He will have the victory in the end anyway.

PRAYER – Father, let my thoughts always be focused on Jesus who pleads for me.I praise You, Father, for helping me to face up to difficult situations.

MARCH 18th

Psalm 23v1-6   Isaiah 53v6   John 10v1-11

The shepherd knows that his flock of sheep need good pasture and the best is often found on the high country. To reach these pastures may involve going through a deep valley where the sun seldom penetrates. He watches over them all the way.

There will be many occasions when you will go through valley experiences. Do you sometimes call out to the Good Shepherd for His guidance and understanding? The air seems dark and still and you sometimes get anxious. All the time Jesus, the Good Shepherd, knows about your inner feelings and what is good for you. He knows where He is taking you and when you get through the valley and reach the rich pastures, you will have cause to rejoice.

PRAYER – Father, please help me to understand that You have a plan for me and want to make sure that I reach the rich pasture after I have passed through the dark valley.

MARCH 19th

Malachi 3v10   Romans 6v11-13   2Timothy 2v15

A collection of medical equipment, forceps etc in the operating theatre are no use unless they are used by the surgeon to relieve some ones suffering.

It is good to remember that we are just 'containers' or 'instruments' through which Jesus can operate. Have you asked Jesus to operate through your life? He will produce strength, love and courage if you will let Him. Thus He will prepare you and use you to help other people in need. As an 'instrument' you are specially designed for a specific purpose and as such, Jesus will expect to use you. Do not envy others but concentrate on the gift God has given you.

PRAYER – Father, I bow to Your complete control in Jesus and I offer my life to be used in Your service, through the gift You have given me, so that I can help folk in the place of Your appointment for me.

MARCH 20th

Ephesians 5v8-11   1Peter 2v9   1John 1v5-7

When the lights go out without a reason, it usually means that something has caused the connections to fail, like a faulty light bulb. By turning on the correct trip switch, the lights should come on again.

Think about light today. God is light; Jesus is light. Does your light shine today in the name of Jesus? Do not block out that light. It is easy to be bogged down with cares and problems to cause a 'break down.' When this happens, the love of Jesus cannot shine through. Call to Him and He will intercede to the Father on your behalf. Then the wonderful light of God will shine through again to overcome any particular difficulty you may have.

PRAYER – Father, I want Your light to shine through me. Take my life and let it be so consecrated to You that Your light will be an encouragement to all my contacts each day.

MARCH 21st

1Chronicles 29v12-13   Psalm 18v31-32   Isaiah 40v28-31

The ropes used to tow boats need to be very strong. The test comes when they are put to use, especially if the boat is stuck.

Jesus understands every detail of how you feel. He knows how far you can go without cracking up. Do you sometimes feel you have reached the limit? Turn to the Word of God and you will find encouragement there to lift you up. Do not fear or be troubled when you cannot tackle a task. If you are in the will of God, He will make it possible and fill your heart with joy because you have 'made it.' Praise will keep you victorious and Satan will have no power to hold you, providing you put your life under the control of Jesus.

PRAYER – Father, I find such encouragement and strength in Your Word and I thank You that Jesus will always guide me along the right path.

MARCH 22nd

1 Corinthians 15v57-58   Ephesians 6v19-20   Philippians 4v13

When we receive good news, the first thing we want to do is to share with someone. We are so thrilled and excited.

Do you have a real desire to make Jesus known? People you meet day by day should know that He lives by observing your attitude and actions. You can only do this when you are walking in His presence by faith. Satan will always try to create havoc in everything you do, disturbing your thoughts and actions. Rest in the Lord and receive His strength. He alone will protect you. Always be on guard and really believe that the Lord is constantly watching over you. Stay on the victory side, serving Jesus and bringing glory to His name.

PRAYER – Father, I praise You for the complete assurance that I am constantly under Your care and protection, being strengthened and prepared for the task You have planned for me to do.

MARCH 23rd

Exodus 34v29   Matthew 5v14-16   Ephesians 5v8

When an important procession or royalty are to pass through the town, barriers are erected along the route to keep back the crowds or possible intruders.

Do you ever put up barriers that tend to stop Jesus shining through your life? As children of the living God, you need to let His life radiate in all you do and say. Do not let the clouds break through the barriers to obliterate God's love. It is not easy because so many things overshadow you from time to time, but you must keep going, keep radiant and bring joy and pleasure to those who watch you, that they may react to your radiance.

PRAYER – Father, clouds do tend to block the sunshine of Your love from time to time, but thank you when the sun breaks through and I can praise You and share Your love with others.

MARCH 24th

Matthew 17v20-21   Luke 1v37&45   Romans 4v18-24

Those who spend time helping in refugee situations are confronted with difficulties that they did not anticipate. For many this situation gives them a very negative reaction.

It is very necessary for you to be positive in your thinking. To plead with Jesus is one thing but you must believe what you are asking and not be distracted by difficult situations. Do you have faith that can remove mountains? Abraham went all the way, God honoured his faith and things really happened. It is so easy to let Satan creep in to say, 'Don't be ridiculous, that can't be so.' Don't let your faith falter. Trust, be not afraid, rejoice in the Lord and praise Him for answers yet to come.

PRAYER – Father, forgive me for the doubts that creep into my thoughts. I know You hear me; I know You will answer. Please give me patience and keep me positive.

MARCH 25th

Psalm 123v1-2   Matthew 28v16-20   Colossians 3v23-24

When blind persons own specially trained guide dogs, they know that the dog will never leave them to manage on their own. In the same way, the dog knows that his master or mistress will always take care of him.

When you hand your life over to Jesus, you will know that you have a responsibility to serve your Master. In the same way you can be sure that He will take care of you. Do you doubt the Lord when He so clearly points out the fact that He needs your help? It is all in Scripture. Keep focused on Him and capture the reflection of His peace. Move from day to day in complete confidence, understanding the needs of your Master.

PRAYER – Father, thank you for the privilege of serving Jesus and for the fact that Jesus is in control of my life. Please help me to keep close to Him in all I say and do.

MARCH 26th

Matthew 7v11   1Timothy 6v17   1Peter 1v8

Nature is responsible for giving us so many good gifts; fruit, vegetables, beautiful flowers and trees, animals and magnificent views over land and sea.

God gives us so much in so many ways; His love, peace and joy. Are you conscious of His goodness in your life? Remember however, that He wants you to share His gifts. To equip you with the necessary ability to do this, He will have to mould and train you. This may not be an easy part of your life, but it is a very necessary part. God knows what He is doing. Just keep going, love the gifts that God provides and thank Him with praises and a grateful heart. All good gifts around us are sent from heaven above.

PRAYER – Father, I am so grateful for Your many gifts of love, peace, joy and strength. Help me to be 'in tune' and constantly aware of Your goodness.

MARCH 27th

Psalm 32v8   Isaiah 49v15-16   Philippians 4v6

Moving to a new town or village in another part of the country can cause quite a lot of anxiety. New district, new home and new friends. The move itself is quite an ordeal.

Why do you need to be anxious? Take the Word of God and read how He promises to guide you and protect you when you trust in Jesus. You can have no greater assurance than this, but you still tend to be anxious about certain things or situations. You must keep Satan at bay so that he can have no hold upon you. Trust God, He will not forget you. What He says He means.

PRAYER – Father, I come close to You for reassurance that You love me and will keep me from being anxious when I believe sincerely what I read in Your Word.

MARCH 28th

Isaiah 40v28-31   James 1v2-7   1Peter 5v8-9

When a moving herd of antelope move for hours over the open grounds of an African safari park, they finish up in a state of exhaustion then rest before the next move. It is at this time that they are likely to be attacked by lion.

When you are tired and weary, Satan will find an easy hunting ground, so beware! Do you find it easy to be tempted when you are tired? Remember, it is at times like this that God promises strength and courage when you trust Jesus to take over the situation. You have no need to doubt His Word, in fact it is wrong to give one thought to doubting. Jesus will not force Himself upon you, so if you chose to face problems alone, you will have to face the consequences.

PRAYER – Father, when I am tired I will turn to You, then call for Jesus to 'take over' to guide me and give me wisdom. I long to reveal Your love but I need that extra strength that You alone can give to me.

MARCH 29th

Proverbs 3v11-12   Jeremiah 10v23-24   Hebrews 12v1-2

Young cadets training for military service have to stick to a rigid programme if they want to enter into active service. It is not easy and discipline overrules any misbehaviour.

This life is just one big training programme preparing us for active service in the name of the Lord. You cannot expect to find the training easy all the time. Do you have any doubts about your training programme? Quite a lot you will not understand but persevere and obey instructions. Keep your eyes upon what you are training for, constantly looking to the Lord for encouragement. Always be ready to learn, then you will experience joy and praise as you advance.

PRAYER – Father, It is so easy for me to get despondent and want to give up my training when the way becomes difficult. Forgive me in my failings and help me to realise what all Your training will mean to me when I really 'stick to it.'

MARCH 30th

Psalm 27v4-5   James 4v7-10   1Peter 5v7

Visiting a particularly beautiful garden thrills us because everywhere seems to be full of goodness. No weeds, lush looking vegetation and beautiful flowers. This could not be so without a faithful, conscientious Gardener.

Jesus can only give you goodness and however much you are attracted away from the things of God, you cannot give in to them if Jesus is always in your thinking. Are you always alert to what Jesus is saying to you? Do you respond when He 'pulls out the weeds?' Jesus will only allow so much of ungodly thoughts to tempt you. He will feed you to strengthen you and give you greater faith. So you will develop and blossom and give pleasure because of the beauty of Jesus radiating through your life.

PRAYER – Father, Your love passes all understanding and I thank you that You tend and care for me to enable that love to bring pleasure to others.

MARCH 31st

Luke 12v22-31   Philippians 2v3-8   Philippians 4v19

In many poor countries the needs are great and the people are destitute. Wages are poor, jobs are few and folks just drift through life. We in the more prosperous countries need to help.

God knows all about your needs and often they are not really needs at all. Do you get anxious about what you think you need or are you thinking about your own wishes? Do not be anxious but trust God to supply all that is necessary. He will not supply what is not necessary, so you should not be disappointed if you do not always receive all you ask for. There will be a good reason. Think instead of the needs of others for there are so many spiritually hungry people. Help them to find Jesus.

PRAYER – Father, thank you that I can always trust You to know my necessary needs. Give me a desire to think of the needs of others and help me to understand why You do not always answer my requests.

APRIL

APRIL 1ˢᵗ

Nehemiah 8v9-10   Habakkuk 3v17-18 pt   Romans 8v28

Sometimes the spring is not as warm as we expect it to be. There are late frosts, heavy rain and strong winds. Creation tends to ignore this. The time has come for the new plant shoots to emerge and emerge they will, even if conditions are not normal.

You cannot pretend to find it easy to praise God when things are weighing heavily upon you. The Lord, in His Word, reminds you that whatever happens to you, any circumstance or situation is good for you. Do you believe this? You love God so you should praise Him for problems, because those things are for your benefit and you will be strengthened. You have a task to do and you should do it, regardless of circumstances, with joy in your heart.

PRAYER – Father, I trust You even when the sun has stopped shining and I want to praise You for the experience I shall gain. Thank you for trusting me.

APRIL 2ⁿᵈ

Matthew 24v4-8; v14   Matthew 24v30-31   2Peter 3v8-13

In the cool of a summer evening a spectacular firework display following a magnificent orchestral presentation, attracts many people in an atmosphere of glorious entertainment.

When Jesus returns, everyone will be filled with a wonderful glory. This thought should overrule any difficult or disturbing situation you may experience at the moment. Do you have any particular problem that is upsetting you at the moment? Your main priority now is to think and prepare or alert others of that wonderful time when Jesus will return to planet earth. It's as simple as that. Continue your service for the Lord, but be alert. No one knows the time. It may not be in your life time but it will happen, Scripture tells us and we need to be ready when it does.

PRAYER – Father, it is so exciting to know that Your Son, Jesus, will be returning one day to sort out this troubled world. Help me to be faithful and serve You by alerting others to listen and believe.

APRIL 3rd

Psalm 90v1,2,4   Psalm 91v14-16   Luke 11v1-10

You will always find crowds at a busy airport waiting for friends or relatives to arrive. Time seems to be endless but then the moment arrives and, 'there they are!' What excitement and happy reunions.

Time seems eternal when you are waiting for something to happen. It doesn't improve the situation to read in the Scriptures that a thousand years is like tomorrow with the Lord. Are you waiting for an answer to your prayer? It could be years before His will is revealed and that's a long time by earthly standards. Maybe you are praying for a loved one to come to Jesus and it never seems to happen. Don't be impatient. God promises to answer prayer; He will not fail, but it may take a little time. When it does, what rejoicing there will be both in heaven and on earth.

PRAYER – Father, forgive my restlessness and help me to realise that you have everything under control, even if I cannot understand how everything will eventually work out.

APRIL 4th

Psalm 37v5-7a   Galatians 5v22   Colossians 1v11-12

Watching fishermen sitting on the riverside with rods fixed and nothing happening, makes one realise how patient they have to be as they sit and wait.

When you consider how obstinate and doubting you can be, you will begin to realise how much patience God has with you. He gently persuades and encourages you through His Word. How often do you find His patience in the Scriptures? Do not pass by His call to you, but search for His guidelines and be patient in all you undertake in His name.

PRAYER – Father, I need to be more patient as I wait for You to guide me into the place you have for me to minister and witness in Your name. As I wait, please help me to relax in Your love.

APRIL 5th

Psalm 119v9-11   John 16v33   Philippians 1v20-21

The sea is powerful, majestic and beautiful. When it is calm it laps gently on the sea shore. When it is rough it leaps and roars. But when confronted by a volcanic eruption,   it erupts in no uncertain terms and causes havoc, such as in the tsunami of 2004.

You may perhaps find it easy to carry on in your own strength when all is going well in your Christian life, but when you come up against difficulties, what do you do and how do you feel? You need to be conscious of Jesus' presence, not occasionally when problems arise but at all times. He is always with you anyway, but He does urge you to have contact with Him. Spend more time in prayer and search the Scriptures for fresh contact daily. Don't cause havoc in your witness but show forth the love, strength and calm of Jesus in your life and witness with others.

PRAYER – Father, I want my life to show Your love, beauty and strength and bring pleasure to folk. Help me not to overwhelm them in my enthusiasm.

APRIL 6th

2 Timothy 2v21   Hebrews 4v15-16   Hebrews 10v19-23

Champions training for a specific sport have to keep to a regular programme. They need to be continually guided by the trainer in order to keep up their strength and concentration.

It is essential that you are constantly coming to the Throne of God, so that you may receive strength and grace for your daily training programme. Do you come to God each day in prayer and praise? Drawing near you will find security and guidance. It is so important to be absolutely certain that you have this security. Now your work will prove that God is in full control. You are preparing to be a vessel through which God can work His purposes out. You must keep the vessel clean.

PRAYER – Father, I want my life to radiate Your love. I know I am a vessel through which You can operate. Help me to be what You want me to be.

APRIL 7th

Joshua 1v8-9   Psalm 32v8-10   Psalm 119v105

Students, in whatever subject they are studying, need to spend time reading books of instruction and learning. If they ignore this part of their training they will not be able to advance very far.

The Word of God reveals His plan and purpose for your life. Do you spend time each day searching the Scriptures for guidance and inspiration? When you feel particularly tired, words of Scripture can be a great help and comfort. Often it is necessary for you to come to this point of exhaustion before God can take you and mould you as He wants, otherwise 'self' tries to take over and that means God cannot penetrate into your life as He wants to do. Do not ignore reading His Word where you will find encouragement and be inspired to go forward to serve a living God.

PRAYER – Father, thank you for Your Word. May I never turn away from the guidance it gives me as I seek to follow the way You have planned for me.

APRIL 8th

Isaiah 58v11   Luke 11v9-13   Philippians 4v19

When it comes to baking, it is essential to have a supply of ingredients. The one who is cooking will produce all that is necessary, otherwise the end result will not be very appetising.

Whatever is necessary for you, God will supply. Do you sometimes ask Him for something that is not really necessary, or try to cut out items that are necessary? If you do, the balance will be upset and you will not be able to serve God in the way He has planned for you. Jesus will always be helping you if you will let Him. He will make things clear and satisfy you with the love that overcomes all differences and doubts. Then you will rejoice in all the necessities supplied.

PRAYER – Father, I do not always think before I ask. I get tempted in my desires for what I consider necessities. Please help me to recognise what You think necessary.

APRIL 9th

Joshua 1v16   John 14v25-27   1Peter 5v7

A young horse can be very unpredictable and first contacts with humans can be very frightening. But with gentle training and loving care, the animal will tame and begin to rely upon his owner.

God has His seal upon you and will take care of you if you will let Him. Are you prepared to let God control your life? It is easy to be anxious and afraid as you travel through life, but if you accept the fact that God has a plan and a purpose in every situation and circumstance He permits you to experience, then you will begin to enter into life with enthusiasm. In the power of God's Holy Spirit in your life, you will be filled with peace, comfort and joy. Trust, have confidence and fear not.

PRAYER – Father, thank you that You accept me as I am, despite my faults and failures, doubts and fears. It is so comforting and encouraging to know that You care. Thank you for helping me in my unbelief.

APRIL 10th

Genesis 1v11-13   1Chronicles 16v31-34   Psalm 103v1-5

In the heart of London there are some lovely gardens. There are delightful flower beds and magnificent trees. Birds sing and there is a feeling of happiness everywhere. But all around the garden the traffic roars and the streets are crowded.

You are surrounded by the things of the world; you are also surrounded by nature. Are you aware that God created the beauty of nature, surrounded as it is by all the hustle and bustle of a busy and disturbed world? Things that the world call 'things to give us pleasure' are created by man and do not have the same significance. You've got to live with them, but be positive about your choice and requirements and do not be influenced by worldly remarks and opinions. Enjoy the creatures and birds; the trees and the flowers and glorious views. In so doing, you will come close to the God of creation and these things will give you more pleasure than any worldly 'thing of pleasure.'

PRAYER – Father, for the beauty of the earth I give You thanks. I praise You for all living things, the pleasure and praise that fills my heart.

APRIL 11th

Genesis 15v1   Matthew 6v1-4   Ephesians 2v8-10

When a big event takes place, many people are involved. Those in the lead are probably well known and prominent, but there will be a team of people in the background planning and preparing. So often they are unknown and unsung heroes in the important part they play.

How easy it is to boast or desire recognition and reward. Do you look for rewards in your service for the Lord? It is human nature in a sense, but Jesus tells us to stop such thoughts. Keep close to Him and you will only want to boast about Jesus. If you do not go along with this idea it proves that you are not close enough to Him. Each morning claim Satan bound by the power of Jesus. Love your Lord and praise Him as He moves you forward and guides you humbly in your duties and responsibilities.

PRAYER – Father, keep me in the hollow of Your hand so that I enjoy doing Your will and do not seek reward other than the heavenly reward to come, providing I am obedient to Your heavenly command. Please help me, Lord.

APRIL 12th

Luke 10v25-37   Romans 7v4   Galatians 5v22-24

Recently the RSPCA were involved in one of the most terrible cases of cruelty to animals they had ever experienced. Horses and dogs had been locked up in a stable; the owner had gone. The RSPCA were faced with dead or sick horses, starving dogs and terrible filth everywhere.

We are all humans and as such, we cannot avoid coming up against the tragedies in our sinful world. Do you find the worldly attractions grip your attention too much? Remember that when you ask Jesus to control your life, you must make room for Him. This may mean sorting out a few things. Do not forget your responsibilities and take care of those who are your contacts, giving loving care and concern. Reflect the glory of Jesus just as far as this is possible.

PRAYER – Father, I want to be more like Jesus and I want my life to reveal His love in all I do and say. But I will need Your help, Your strength and dedicated determination.

APRIL 13th

Isaiah 58v11   Luke 11v1-10   Hebrews 13v8 and 20-21

With winter past, the time to think about holidays is beginning to emerge, where to go, what to take and how to travel etc. It can become confusing as we try to work it all out from a pile of brochures and suggestions.

Sometimes you may work and even struggle to fulfil all that God has called you to do, but seem to be getting nowhere. Do you sometimes feel this way? You need to pray continually and do not be dismayed if no answer seems to be forthcoming. God does hear but he wants you to keep praying, fixing your thoughts constantly upon Jesus, relying on Him to encourage and guide you. The day will come when the answer to your prayers will be revealed. You will be amazed what God has in store for you.

PRAYER – Father, my heart is full of praise and thanksgiving that You always know what is best for me. Help me to be patient as I wait for the answer to my prayers. Knowing that you have the best and right answer already planned.

APRIL 14th

Matthew 7v13-14   James 1v12   1Peter 1v1-8

There is only one way that is correct in a maze. The path looks the same but if you go the wrong way you come to a dead end and will have to return to the main path and try again.

When you go about your daily tasks it is easy to 'take the wrong turning' by tackling things that are not so important in your Christian life. Do you realise that Jesus is always by your side? He enables you to go about your faith in the right way if you will rely upon Him. Be prepared to change course and be open to His will. If you 'get down' Jesus will understand and will encourage you. God allows experiences like this in your life, but they are for your good in the long run. You have nothing to fear.

PRAYER – Father, thank you for all your concern for me. Please give me the determination I need to let Jesus take control.

APRIL 15th

Psalm 2v8   Luke 12v22-26   Philippians 4v12-13

Birds of the air have no fear of the present or the future concerning their daily needs. Wild animals have the same attitude, reptiles and fish too. Somehow, they know their needs will be supplied.

We all need to consider humility. It is so important for you to be completely satisfied with Jesus, not yearning for rich possessions or important positions. Are you content to follow the way Jesus leads? Jesus never concentrated on 'things'; He concentrated on people and you must do the same. There are so many people to help. Concentrate on how Jesus wants you to be involved. Quality of character is far more important than what you possess.

PRAYER – Father, I have the wonderful assurance of knowing that You will always provide all that I need. I have no anxiety therefore, over my possessions. Praise You, Lord.

APRIL 16th

John 16v33   2Corinthians 4v16   1Timothy 6v11-15

Put an egg in the microwave without pricking it and it will not be long before it will explode. The pressure was too much for it.

Do you reach times when you feel that the testing you are experiencing is just more than you can take? For some reason God has brought you to this point and you need to come close to Him to find out His purposes for your life. Now He can get your full attention. Surrender to Him, search His Word and be faithful in prayer. Be filled with His Spirit so that He can use you. Now you will overflow with joy and peace.

PRAYER – Father, You know the best for me and I yield my life to You in praise and glory as You direct my life and make me useful in Your service.

APRIL 17th

Matthew 28v20   John 16v13   Acts 2v25

When a new bathroom is fitted into the house it has to have all the necessary fittings to make it functional and practical. Once the bathroom is installed it is there for always for your use or for others.

What a wonderful fact it is to know that as you ask Jesus into your life, He will always be there. Are you always conscious of His presence each day? You must therefore accept the fact that He will decide the right things for you; where to go and what to do. Be thankful that He overrules all your thoughts and desires. You may not understand His ways at the time; you may be disappointed. But remember, each guiding thought is necessary to complete the whole way of your life.

PRAYER – Father, I thank You for Jesus who guides my thinking and planning and is so understanding. I want the construction of my life to fit in to Your desires for me.

APRIL 18th

Psalm 19v12-13   Matthew 6v33-34   1Corinthians 3v16-17

When we own a car it is our responsibility to look after it. A regular check at the garage, an MOT, a tyre and oil check. All regular jobs to be attended to, but it is our responsibility to make sure these checks are carried out.

Our bodies are temples of the Holy Spirit and it is our responsibility to look after them. Do you have a daily routine for your lifestyle and concern for both your physical and spiritual life? Remember Jesus is in your life if you have put your trust in Him and you need to keep things in order so that He can take full possession. You need to have a regular check of every detail of your life but it is your responsibility to bring every area under His control. Your reward will be worth every effort.

PRAYER – Father, I need to keep my life clean and in order. Thank you that Jesus will help me to do this.

APRIL 19th

Psalm 26v7   Acts 20v24   Colossians 1v27-29

When we receive some good news we can't wait to share it with someone. Sometimes the recipient is excited too, but sometimes they do not seem to respond as enthusiastically as we expect them to.

As you pass through this world you should be bursting with enthusiasm to share Jesus with everyone. Do you long to share all that Jesus means to you? Think of all the many blessings He has bestowed upon you and long to share them with others. Explain what it means to walk with Jesus. Some people may not appear to be responsive, but if they are going through a 'rough patch' you can be such an encouragement to them.

PRAYER – Father, thank you for the opportunities You give to me, so that I get excited and can be helpful to others in need of Your mercy and grace. Help me to be bold and sincere in my approach.

APRIL 20th

Philippians 4v4-7   Colossians 3v1-4   1Peter 5v6-7

Keeping in contact with business concerns these days is not as simple as just writing a letter. Life today is so technical and complicated. E-mail, websites, computers, mobile phones etc.

It is so easy to get caught up with the complexities that the world has to offer today. Do you sometimes feel overwhelmed by anxiety over something? Listen to Jesus and He will reassure you that there is no need for you to be overwhelmed by circumstances. You are being prepared for future days. Just now you have to live in the world and adapt to modern developments. You have a responsibility to share His love, His care and concern in what ever way He guides, either ancient or modern. Don't be put off by technicalities.

PRAYER – Father, please equip me with the ability to face up to problems that confront me each day. Thank you that Jesus is always ready to help me.

APRIL 21st

Colossians 1v10-14   2 Thessalonians 1v11-12   2 Peter 3v3-9

Looking round a busy shopping centre we see so many people bustling about and they all seem so busy. What would happen to them if there was a sudden emergency; a raid, earthquake or overpowering storm of some kind?

We all have a responsibility in our Christian lives to share our faith amongst so many who need the love of God in their lives. Have you friends or family for whom you have concern? You will need to equip yourself with all that it takes to be bold and faithful in prayer. Apparent impossibilities can occur in the name of Jesus. Don't attempt to approach people on spiritual issues in your own strength; just have faith and believe. You will be conscious of abundant blessings in the power of the Holy Spirit.

PRAYER – Father, help me to witness for You as Jesus calls me to do in the place and amongst the people You lead me to today. May I have deep concern for the many people who are in so much need of You.

APRIL 22nd

1 Corinthians 9v16   Romans 3v23-24   2 Timothy 2v1-3

Water in a kettle will keep boiling so long as it is in contact with a power source. When the contact is cut the water stops boiling.

It is only by close contact with the grace of God that you are what you are. What does this grace mean to you? It means that Jesus died to save you from the sins and mistakes in your life. He then placed the power of His Spirit within you, enabling you to 'boil' in your service and witness for Him. If you ignore these facts you will cease to operate as you should. Let the love of God and the real meaning of His grace soak into your soul and give you the desire to 'boil' for Jesus.

PRAYER – Father, I praise You for Your wonderful gift of grace. Thank you for Jesus who gives me the power and enthusiasm to 'boil.'

APRIL 23rd

1 Samuel 3v9-10   Psalm 119v105   James 1v22-25

If you own a cat no doubt you become attached to it. Also the cat becomes attached to you. If you ignore it from time to time, the cat will remind you that it is there by meowing and rubbing against your legs. You can't ignore it.

Wherever we are, the Lord is there too, whether we acknowledge His presence or not. He is there, longing that we will listen to Him. Are you listening to what the Lord has to say? You may believe in God and acknowledge Jesus, but have you committed your whole life to Him? In so doing, you will find peace and comfort and joy. He knows your innermost thoughts and His love for you is continuous. Put your trust in Him and consider your responsibilities to care for those who need the love of God too.

PRAYER – Father, I need Your presence in my life. Encourage me by Your Word, and may I realise my responsibilities to others too.

APRIL 24th

Psalm 9v10   Proverbs 3v5-6   Romans 15v13

There are times when we all have to visit the dentist. We have to trust the dentist to discover any faults and put them right for us.

We all need to have a much greater trust in the Lord. How much do you trust God to do what He says in His Word? It is easy to say, 'Oh, the Lord will help me.' It is another thing to be absolutely certain and really mean it. Why do you have such doubts? When you are certain of God's authority and power, you will let the Holy Spirit take over and then you will have no doubts.

PRAYER – Father, please forgive me for my human uncertainty and give me the desire to put my whole trust in you through the power of Your Spirit.

APRIL 25th

Psalm 31v3   Isaiah 41v13   John 5v30

If you are having a complicated problem with your computer, what a comfort and relief it is when a friend offers to sort out the problem.

Jesus was ready and willing to help His Father to carry out His wishes and plans. Are you willing to help and follow God in fitting into His plans for you? Jesus did not complain, but responded to His Father's wishes. In the same way Jesus will come alongside you and help to sort out your problem. Concentrate on your task as He guides you. You will be rewarded with a great sense of praise in your heart.

PRAYER – Father, I want to be sure that I am doing my work as You have planned. I am so grateful for Jesus who helps me understand.

APRIL 26th

Daniel 3v16-18   1Corinthians 16v13   1 John 5v4

Properties are normally built on a firm foundation. Owners purchasing properties normally accept a sound building in faith.

Faith is the base upon which you must build your Christian life. Do you sometimes long for more faith? You need to have a feeling of complete security in Jesus, so spend time in His presence. The Bible is full of stories about so many who had faith in the Lord. It is not always easy, because Satan will step in when you doubt, and try to lure you away from your trust in God. Do not be distracted but be encouraged to follow Jesus, the solid foundation upon which you can build up your faith.

PRAYER – Father, please help me to understand the true meaning of faith. Give me courage and enthusiasm to follow Jesus, the firm foundation upon which I can build my faith.

APRIL 27th

Psalm 27v5   Psalm 37v3-5   Psalm 91v1-2

During the Second World War Anderson air-raid shelters were erected in many town and city centres. Somehow one felt a sense of security to rush for the shelters when the sirens sounded.

It is so important to feel secure in your faith. Do you have doubts about your security and your future? If you do feel secure, make it known by sharing with others who have doubts. It would be unkind not to do so. Show Jesus in your life by word or deed, through the light of His love and protection. He is your shelter from all fear and harm, the One in which you feel secure.

PRAYER – Father, I want to reveal Jesus in my life and help those who have doubts about their future and need the security that can only be found in Jesus.

APRIL 28th

Exodus 15v1-6   Psalm 71v8   Ephesians 1v11-14

There are times when a special occasion or reunion occurs. Everyone is happy and are ready to sing and rejoice as they celebrate, forgetting all their problems and other concerns for a while.

We are told to praise the Lord in every situation. Are there times when you find it difficult to praise the Lord? Turn your eyes upon Jesus knowing that He will bring such peace and love that you will automatically want to praise and rejoice. When answers do not seem to come to your prayers, do not be despondent. God is in control and He only wants the best for you. Think of occasions in Scripture when the Israelites praised God with Moses when they were in the wilderness. They often passed through times of disappointments and upsets, but God always provided for them.

PRAYER – Father, forgive me for my impatience. Now receive my praise as I realise Your loving care and concern for me. I rejoice in the Lord my God.

APRIL 29th

Proverbs 3v11-12   Isaiah 1v19   Hebrews 12v11

Obedience is one point that is very important if things are to run smoothly in life. A false step against advice can cause a severe crisis and utter disruption.

What a difference it makes in your Christian life when you are obedient. Have you always tried to do what you have been asked to do? It is sometimes easier to think you have a better way of doing something other than the way God asks. If you are not obedient to His requests you will have to go through a period of discipline in the form of difficult periods or situations. Jesus loves you and will help you. He wants you to be a witness, and His discipline will give you a greater sense of responsibility and trust. Don't disappoint Him.

PRAYER – Father, I want to be obedient but I do not always find it easy. I will listen to Jesus who is always ready to help me. Please humble me enough to respond to Him.

APRIL 30th

1 Chronicles 28v8-10   1Peter 5v7   Revelation 7v17

The nose of a dog is more sensitive than its owners nose. He also has a greater ability to sense danger or unusual situations. It is wise to react to his sensitivity.

We must always accept the fact that God knows best, even if we think otherwise. Do you love God enough to know that His plans for you are the best? You may feel that things are unnatural, but God's plans always make sense in the long run. He is always in control. Do not mind criticism or ridicule. All this will strengthen your character and cause you to draw nearer to the Lord. Rejoice in the peace and security He will bring. Cast all your cares on Him, for He cares for you.

PRAYER – Father, I desire the presence and power of Your Spirit to be seen in me, but I need to rely upon Your guidance to keep me from harm and danger. Please make me sensitive in my walk with You,

MAY

MAY 1st

Isaiah 26v3-4   John 14v27   Romans 5v1-5

Magnificent scenery across rolling hills, and flourishing fields and woodlands, create an atmosphere of peace and tranquillity. A sudden storm disturbs that peace and reveals a picture of turmoil.

It is difficult to explain or understand the true meaning of peace. Do you feel really peaceful yourself? Day by day you face a world in chaos, saturated with danger and fear. People will ask you, 'Why does God allow these things to happen?' It is man's fault not God's fault. He wants you to enjoy a beautiful world. Things are only as they are because Satan was allowed to enter the world way back in the days of Adam and Eve. Eventually God had to sacrifice His only Son as a way of release for you and me. But as you rejoice in your salvation consider those who still need to understand.

PRAYER – Father, thank you for the beauty of this wonderful world. I rejoice in such love that passes all understanding. Help me to share Your love with folks, through all the storms of life that surround us.

MAY 2nd

Acts 20v1-2   Romans 15v4   Hebrews 10v22-23

Any sports competition is a centre for enthusiastic response from supporters, as they cheer their choice of team or individual. This in turn, encourages the participants.

Words of assurance and encouragement from God's Word are a wonderful antidote for human worries and anxieties. Are you anxious about anything or anyone in particular? Are you encouraging anyone? Read God's Word and see how many of His followers came up against difficulties, but how they were encouraged by God. Let the love of Jesus penetrate into your very being. This will be the encouragement and assurance you need to overcome all your anxieties and stimulate you as you follow the way He leads.

PRAYER – Father, I need Your encouragement every day and I thank You for Your precious Word. Lead me on as You assure me of Your continual support.

MAY 3rd

Isaiah 60v1   Romans 15v13   Philippians 2v15-16a

It will soon be time for the season of country fairs. They are all the same, displays, stalls, animals, people and activities of all kinds. Where do you go first?

Human thoughts and desires surround you every day. What do you do about these things? You need to 'clear the way' so that Jesus may come into your life and fill you with a greater desire to think His thoughts. Be filled with His Spirit so that His light can shine forth to penetrate into the hearts of others. Shine Jesus, shine and let me enjoy all the special activities and displays You give for my pleasure.

PRAYER – Father, I pray that I may be so filled with Your Spirit, that all may see Your light and joy shining through me.

MAY 4th

Psalm 31v3   John 16v13   Philippians 4v6-7

These days mobile phones are all the 'rage' and are used everywhere, even linking countries. There is immediate contact.

Although you might not be aware, God is continually speaking to you, trying to guide you in the right direction. Do you listen to Him and daily seek His will for you? You need to come to the point of complete surrender and let God have every part of your life. Jesus wants to help you so that you can give God all the glory, in obedience and love. You have immediate contact with Him through prayer, so make a habit of daily communication. Be patient and willing to let Him have His way.

PRAYER – Father, I want to be where You want me to be, do what You want me to do and say what You want me to say. Help me Lord, to keep in contact.

MAY 5th

Psalm 32v8-10   Romans 15v4-6   Hebrews 12v2-3

In a busy household or office situation for example, it is often necessary to delegate some of the work. If you have been in this situation you will know that you have to chose someone you can trust with the responsibility.

We all need to have more trust in the faith we believe. Do you trust Jesus to guide you each day? This will mean keeping your eyes upon Him and being alert as He leads you onward. Remember Whom you represent and remember your responsibilities. He will give you instructions and you must be faithful to carry them out. If you do not keep in touch with Jesus, you are likely to find yourself closed in by Satan's subtle ways. Watch and pray that you are not drawn away from your responsibilities.

PRAYER – Father, keep me trusting You as I seek to follow Jesus, as He instructs me. Thank you for choosing me and giving me these responsibilities.

MAY 6th

Isaiah 53v1-6   Luke 22v42-44   Hebrews 13v12-15

When we have a medical problem we go to see the doctor. If he advises an operation or some painful treatment, we agree that he knows best and we obey his wishes. How much better we feel afterwards.

Do you ever stop to realise how much Jesus suffered in order to carry out His Father's wishes? He obeyed His Father in order to redeem us from sin. Our physical suffering is only a fraction of what Jesus endured. Because He ascended into heaven after His death, it is possible for His Spirit to enter your life. Jesus is alive, very much alive! Now He is able to take control of your life and guide you into a life of worship and praise, so that you can radiate His love and rejoice with joy unspeakable and full of glory.

PRAYER – Father, when I stop to concentrate, I realise just a little of what Jesus suffered on my behalf. Help me to appreciate His presence in my life so that I can rejoice and be glad.

MAY 7th

Jeremiah 33v6   John 14v27   Revelation 1v17-18

When your money is locked away either in the bank, reliable investment or somewhere safe, you can be sure that it is secure. This results in a sense of peace of mind.

Have you ever considered the complete security you have in God? You have a real shelter in the hollow of His hand, so that whatever man may do or whatever circumstances you face, you have nothing to fear. It is so easy to build up problems, then to be afraid. The moment you realise the security you have in God and the confidence you have in Jesus, that fear will go. A wonderful sense of peace and relaxation will fill your heart.

PRAYER – Father, I am so glad that I have complete security in You. I will not fear what man can do, but will accept the Spirit of Jesus into my heart to protect me from all my fears.

MAY 8th

Deuteronomy 8v15-16   1 Thessalonians 5v21-22   James 1v12

Before buying certain things we usually test them to make sure they are working. If there are doubts we tend to reject the item concerned.

Life is full of testing times and day by day we come up against things that need to be tested before we can confirm that they are reliable. What are you testing out today? You must always accept the testing Jesus wants you to have. Remember, He has promised never to leave you. When the testing is troubling you, accept the encouragement you find in Scripture and remember that He is always watching you, even if you do not realise it. Keep going.

PRAYER – Father, Keep me trusting through times of testing, conscious of Your guiding hand and the comfort of Jesus by my side.

MAY 9th

Matthew 17v20-21   2Corinthians 5v7   Hebrews 11v1-2

When we look up to the sky at night we see the stars and the moon shining brightly. Looking up during the day we cannot see them. Do we have faith to believe that they are still there?

Faith is the essence by which we believe in God. Do you have faith in what you cannot see? It is not easy to have complete faith when you cannot see the way clearly ahead. You want proof and confirmation. But you have to learn to live by what God tells you and promises you through His Son, the Word and the Holy Spirit. You have no grounds to doubt His authority. He has the future planned and relies upon you to follow where He leads. Many circumstances will try to dislodge your faith, but don't be distracted. Trust in the Lord.

PRAYER – Father, I need to have more faith. I commit my activities and thoughts to You. Please help me to follow the way You lead, knowing that You always mean what You say.

MAY 10th

1Corinthians 10v13   1 Peter 5v8-9   Revelation 12v10-11

As we look around our world we see so much fighting and civil strife. God made planet earth for us to enjoy, but so often its peace and beauty is destroyed by man's wickedness and the constant battles for power and position.

Jesus knew what it was like to be in a constant battle with Satan so therefore He knows what it is like for you. Does it trouble you when you are confronted by Satan? Remember, Jesus conquered Satan at Calvary so although you are troubled by his cunning ways, you do not need to fear. Stop to think and realise that Jesus knew all about the suffering and torment from others, but He overcame these things and in His name and with His determination, you can too.

PRAYER – Father, please help me to be confident in Jesus when I am confronted by Satan with His subtle and evil ways. Give me determination to conquer him and to know Your will and purpose for my life.

MAY 11th

John 17v3   Romans 6v23   James 1v16-17

When we eat in a restaurant we believe that the food we are eating is wholesome. We trust the chef to know what he is doing and we enjoy the result.

In this world, when you trust in Jesus and commit your life to Him, you are being saved for eternal life. Are your thoughts geared in that direction? Time spent here is temporary and you will experience a feast of good things as you pass through, because God knows how to give good gifts to His children. Enjoy all He has to offer you in the presence of Jesus and do not be tempted to take any interest in anything that would draw you away from what God has to offer you.

PRAYER – Father, I want to keep in constant touch with You so that I can enjoy all that You have for me to enjoy. Please do not let me be distracted by unacceptable thoughts and actions.

MAY 12th

Jeremiah 31v3   John 15v12-14   2 Corinthians 5v14-15

Have you ever watched the activities of ants? They live together in vast numbers and lead a very active and organised life. Their main object is to help one another, serving in love to one another on an amazing scale.

Love is the basis of our faith. God is love and He is waiting to fill us with His love, and longs for us to love Him too. Do you love God in a really sincere way? God tells you to love others but you cannot truly love others until you commit all of yourself in love to God. Jesus is ready and waiting to penetrate right into your life through His Spirit, but as long as you hold back or block that flow of love, then it is not possible for you to really love others in all sincerity.

PRAYER – Father, I praise You for the privilege of being used as a channel through which your love can flow. Please help me not to block the flow.

MAY 13th

Jeremiah 29v11   Matthew 19v26   1Thessalonians 5v16-18

When we are faced with a selection of broken and muddled maps to sort out or put in order, the task seems quite impossible and we give up. Do we ever consider asking someone to help?

Most of us are really incapable of praying sincerely to God and often we wait until things seem to be impossible. Do you make a habit of coming to God in prayer, whether things are going right or wrong? You need to pray without ceasing in every circumstance. Learn to pray in depth and have faith to believe that God is listening and will deal with whatever situation you are praying about. Behind everything that happens is the Eternal One, who knows the plans He has for you. Jesus is always present to intervene on your behalf. Seek His help.

PRAYER – Father, when I become weak You reveal Yourself in power. Please help me to achieve the possible from the seemingly impossible situations I face from time to time.

MAY 14th

Isaiah 58v11   Psalm 58v11   Hebrews 12v2

To place some beautiful crystal and exotic china amongst a collection of old mugs and chipped glasses would look odd. The items would not blend because their styles are quite different.

We all have human characteristics, all look and act differently but can all be drawn into the things that this world has to offer. How do you fit into the world situation? Praise the Lord that He has made a way so that you do not have to be drawn into the worldly mould. The condition is that you observe the way of escape by keeping your eyes fixed upon Jesus who is waiting to direct you. We are all made differently but we all have a specific use in the world. Seek to be useful and victorious in Jesus.

PRAYER – Father, thank you that You have a place for me in the world, whether important or unimportant. Thank you that Jesus is always ready to guide me into the right situation.

MAY 15th

Acts 1v8   Romans 8v16-17   James 5v10-11

A broken leg causes not only a lot of discomfort and often pain, but it can also be very inconvenient for getting around.

Sometimes physical suffering prevents you from doing all you would like to do or plan. Are you suffering from a disability that prevents you from all you wish to be in your Christian life? You need to overcome the inconvenience by concentrating on God's desire for you. He knows all about your disabilities but He also knows what you are capable of doing and will give you the ability to concentrate on that special gift. Remember, God never goes back on His Word.

PRAYER – Father, my disabilities frustrate me sometimes but I know You understand. Please give me the will power to share Your loving understanding in my daily witness.

MAY 16th

Hebrews 10v35-36   1Peter 1v8-9   1Peter 5v7

On the whole animals like company. They like to be together and to share experiences in a relaxed atmosphere that gives them pleasure.

Whatever we do in our Christian lives, it is so important to keep close to Jesus. Are you always aware that Jesus is right beside you? Remember to tell Him all that is happening in your life, the difficult moments and the happy, exciting moments. It will make you feel so good just to be able to 'chat' with Someone who is really listening close beside you. Never trust yourself alone in your Christian walk; you must have genuine guidance and help. Companionship is very important and encouraging and Jesus will never leave you.

PRAYER – Father, I cannot see Jesus but I know He is just beside me, because you tell me so. Therefore I will go forward in confidence. Thank you, Lord, for Your loving care.

MAY 17th

Matthew 5v43-48   Luke 6v37-38   1John 3v11

How often have you watched any courting displays amongst particular bird species? The males reveal outstanding displays with elaborate scenes to catch the eye. So often the female is not amused.

It is not good to be so 'holy' that we tend to distract people when we reveal our faith. Do you give people the impression that their 'style' of living is 'out of order?' To be holy means to be really loving, sincere, caring and understanding. It is so easy to take the attitude of 'looking down' on someone who does not see faith in Jesus as you do and therefore it becomes easy to 'condemn' them. When you love God sincerely, you will want to love others in a natural way because you really care.

PRAYER – Father, give me the love for people that will draw them closer to You and will give them a desire to love Jesus. Make me humble and loving in all I do and say.

MAY 18th

2 Chronicles 35v2   Romans 1v12   Romans 15v4

Children love to be recognised when they do something that is good. They should be encouraged but must realise that results must not involve boasting. They must be taught the difference.

It is encouraging to welcome recognition in the ministry we do for the Lord, but this tends to put God in second place. Do you look for people to praise you for a job well done? To a certain degree you need to be encouraged and this is good, for we are told to encourage one another. But what you do you are doing for the Lord; a task He has called you to do. It stands to reason therefore, that He should have all the glory and praise. However, do not forget to encourage others in their service for Him too.

PRAYER – Father, I am honoured to do the task You have called me to do. Please help me to do it well. To You be the glory, great things You have done.

MAY 19th

Isaiah 9v2   Ephesians 5v8-11   1Peter 2v9

In tropical countries the change from day to night is quite remarkable. One minute it is light and the next minute it is dark. There is no twilight. The same in the morning. One minute dark, then suddenly it is light.

As you offer your life to God, you will suddenly be transformed from darkness to light. Have you found that even your thinking has changed since you first came to know Jesus? To complete the transformation you will need to have the power of His Spirit in your life. You need to be in the full light of God's presence to reveal defects not seen in the darkness. Enjoy the light, rejoice and give thanks, then you will be able to transmit the power and love of God's light into every situation, also amongst other Christian colleagues.

PRAYER – Father, take my life from the darkness and let it be consecrated to You, so that I can be transformed into the light of Your love and cleansed from any defects.

MAY 20th

Psalm 119v105   Romans 13v12   Ephesians 6v10-18

Wherever we go in the UK we need to take protection against the weather which can be most unpredictable. A raincoat will keep us dry and safe from the possibility of heavy rain.

Wherever you go these days along the pilgrim way, you need to be protected from satanic 'rain storms' or danger spots. Will you always think before you step out on a certain project, to make sure you are well protected? In your walk with the Lord, you will need daily protection against any attacks from the evil ways of life. These ways can be subtle, so never leave a crack uncovered. Spend time with the Word of God. This is the armour you need to protect you. Then as you draw near to God, He will draw near to you.

PRAYER – Father, thank you that I can find in Your Word all that is necessary to protect me in my daily walk with You. Your Word is a light to my path and I need to take it in.

MAY 21st

Psalm 18v32   Isaiah 12v2   Isaiah 40v28-31

After a very active day or a particularly energetic ramble, we naturally feel a bit weak, and long to sit and relax with nothing particular to do. We need to be refreshed with food or sleep.

There are times in your Christian life when you will feel weak and incapable and your thinking tends to become negative. Do you have moments like this? In a sense, this is just how God wants you to feel. Now He can take over and mould you into His pattern. In this state you can now be used for the glory of God. He will give you the strength that you need, then when things are in order, you will experience His joy in your life and be able to reflect the love and beauty of Jesus. You will be astonished what will happen.

PRAYER – Father, I am willing to be weak so that Your strength will take over. Take me and use me to bring honour and glory to Your name.

MAY 22nd

Psalm 26v3   Psalm 119v165   Philippians 4v6-7

In the stillness of a summer morning there is an atmosphere of peace. The birds are stretching their tiny wings and the little animals stir. Everywhere is quiet as day slowly emerges into a world of activity.

It is so difficult to experience peace in the world these days. Are there times in your life when you just long for peace? The peace that Jesus gives is unexplainable, but it can fill you with a sense of quiet and relaxation; wonderful! With such peace in your heart, all 'buts and ifs'; problems and trials, seem to be insignificant. To appreciate this peace you must come to a point of utter dependence upon the God of creation, and the quietness of a beautiful morning.

PRAYER – Father, it is so wonderful to know that you can create the beauty of a new morning. In the realisation of this I thank You and praise You for Your unexplainable peace.

MAY 23rd

Matthew 6v13   Mark 14v37-38   1Corinthians 10v13

It is difficult to pass by a magnificent display of delicious looking pastries when you are on a diet. Such a temptation. A strong will is necessary to decline.

How easy it is to fall into temptation. How difficult it is to avoid temptation. Are you constantly reminded of this fact? You want to be faithful in your walk with Jesus and you need to listen to Him more often. He cannot help you if you harbour the wrong thoughts and fall into temptation without a strong desire and determination to keep out of Satan's grip. He will take any opportunity to 'sneak' into your life. Do not be tempted.

PRAYER – Father, let me reveal the power of Jesus in everything. I do not want to fall into temptation, so please help me to be faithful and always put my confidence in Jesus.

MAY 24th

Psalm 81v13   Proverbs 19v20   Mark 9v7

There are times when we are under leadership and need to listen to the one who is trying to explain something special to us. We have to listen if we want to understand.

When your life is under the control of Jesus, you need to listen to what He has to say. Are you sometimes overcome by your own desires? You need to know the difference between your desires and God's desires for your life. To ignore or disobey will disappoint the Lord and then you will be unable to fulfil His purposes for your life. Be alert and listen to your Leader.

PRAYER – Father, it is so easy to make mistakes when I do not keep in close contact with You. Forgive my mistakes and keep me always ready to listen and understand.

MAY 25th

John 14v1-6   2Corinthians 4v17-18   2Thessalonians 2v16-17

The business of moving house can be very traumatic but when one thinks of how a few alterations will improve the whole property, one has something special to look forward to.

When as a believer you follow Jesus, you will have a wonderful future to look forward to; a future in the presence of Jesus in eternity. Do you get excited about the prospect of that glorious future? Any experiences you have now are just times of preparation. There will be alterations and improvements but future thoughts will outweigh any preparation problems. Never have any doubts when you are trusting God.

PRAYER – Father, it is so encouraging to know that You understand my moments of traumatic circumstances. I want to 'get my house in order,' knowing that it is for my future good.

MAY 26th

Matthew 6v33-34   1Peter 1v3-4   Titus 2v11-13

When there is a wedding in the family, this is a special event and much time is spent in preparation, anticipating a time of great excitement and celebration.

Are you looking forward to something special? During your Christian pilgrimage all kinds of special events happen from time to time. It is natural to get excited but often you are the one that is involved in the preparations, so you must expect all kinds of experiences which may cause you to have doubts. Do not be anxious but continue to love and serve the Lord so that His love will overcome any problems. He is in control. Keep your eyes on the future 'special event' and get excited about your eternal destiny. Then anything you have to cope with en route will be possible.

PRAYER – Father, thank you that I have a wonderful future ahead. As I prepare for that, I will accept all the necessary preparation you plan for me on the way.

MAY 27th

Psalm 4v8   Matthew 6v25-34   Hebrews 12v14-15

It is easy to build up a host of problems from one doubt. You may have taken on a new job and it is not easy to fit into new ways of doing things, so one query leads to another.

Do you tend to get anxious and worried over nothing in particular? Life is full of things to worry you and make you anxious. Do not let them, but have complete confidence in the Lord, knowing that He has everything concerning your pathway through life under control. You will always have many things to 'put right' and it will not always be easy to 'get on' with certain people. Show them what Jesus means to you but always remember to act as Jesus guides you to act. Love these folks without argument or resentment. Life will then be so rewarding.

PRAYER – Father, I am so conscious of Your peace in my heart when I follow the pathway you chose for me. Thank you that when I keep close to You, I want to reflect Your love to the folk who tend to have opposite thoughts to mine.

MAY 28th

Psalm 107v28-31   Nahum 1v3-7   1Peter 5v7

When a severe storm is approaching it is usually heralded by a strong wind. Then the clouds gather, the lightning flashes and the thunder roars. It can do untold damage and cause havoc before the rain falls and it passes on. Then the clear up starts.

How do you tackle the inevitable storms of life when they confront you? As they approach, you need to be sure that there is nothing in your life which would hold you back from being all that Jesus wants you to be. The storms are necessary to clear the ground, and this means that you will pass through experiences that may be hard for you to understand. But the end of the storm will bring a freshness which will encourage you and help you to understand.

PRAYER – Father, I am so thrilled that the storm in my life has cleansed away the dross and increased my faith and love for You. Than you for Your constant care.

MAY 29th

Psalm 85v6-10   Matthew 6v5-8   Philippians 4v6

It is not unusual for a child to ask again and again for something he or she wants, but, for some reason, does not receive. Maybe it would not be good for them or maybe there is a delay for a particular reason. They do not understand, so repeat their request.

Do you find yourself continually repeating unanswered prayers? When you do this, it is as if you are reminding God about a certain situation, trying to hurry Him up. He has heard you the first time, so there is no need to keep on worrying. Leave the original prayer request with Him, knowing that He understands completely and will answer in due course in a way that is best for you. It may not be in the way you had in mind, but commune with Jesus and know that the whole situation will be dealt with according to God's plan and purpose for your life.

PRAYER – Father, I'm sorry I tend to be so impatient. I know that You care for me and hear my prayers, but I need to have more faith to realise that in Your love and mercy You will answer in Your own time.

MAY 30th

1Corinthians 9v24-27   1Corinthians 10v24-27   Hebrews 12v1

The future is hidden from us. We plan and prepare for great ideas when we get to retirement days, but so often these ideas never come to fruition.

Do you sometimes wonder what the future holds in store for you? When you have faith and believe what you read in the Word of God, you can be confident that your future is secure. Remember that this life is your training ground and learning centre; a time of preparation for that wonderful future. Share your knowledge with others, alert them and remind them what the future means. Run your race, ignoring some things that would hold you back from doing your best.

PRAYER – Father, I want to take every opportunity of the training available to me as I run this race of faith. I know how important it is to share the resulting love and peace with others as I go.

MAY 31st

John 16 v12-15   James 1v5-6   1John 5v13-15

When you watch a two legged race, possibly at a school sports day function, see how important it is for the two children concerned to move in unison, otherwise they fall and are out of the race.

Do you have doubts in your faith and your daily walk with Jesus? It is absolutely essential that you become completely one with Jesus so that you have no doubts in knowing that He understands all about you. He has your life mapped out in every detail and He will hear you when you 'talk' to Him, because He is right beside you. As He 'talks' back to you, He will make it possible for you to take the right direction. But you must be sensitive to what He guides you to do and say.

PRAYER – Father, it is so wonderful that You have made it possible for Jesus to be with me continually through His Spirit, and to guide me in the right direction if I will listen and respond.

JUNE

JUNE 1st

Psalm 103v1-2   Galatians 5v22-23   Ephesians 4v1-2

As food is sent to relieve the appalling poverty situations in so many parts of the world these days, it must be shared so that everyone has the opportunity to benefit.

Do you share the benefits you have experienced in your Christian life with others who do not know about the love of Jesus? Before God can pour out His blessings upon you, there must be a time when you commit your life fully to Jesus. Then through His Spirit, life will take on a whole new meaning. You will want to share these blessings. Break down the barriers and keep your eyes upon Jesus and His love will flow through you to others. Look for opportunities of service to help others with real joy and love in your heart.

PRAYER – Father, let the love of Jesus be seen in me and keep me trusting in Your power and blessings. May my life be an encouragement to share with others.

JUNE 2nd

Isaiah 55v8-9   Hebrews 10v22-23   1Peter 1v13

When considering a holiday it is necessary to make plans. It is not always possible to keep to them but at least a programme can be arranged, then the plan will become clear.

Every day when you start into your programme do you remember that God cares for you? You have plans but you cannot be sure that they will always be uninterrupted. We must all be prepared for Jesus to return at any time, but still you must continue to carry out the work He has planned for you to do, regardless of occasions that you have not planned. God cares and always has a reason for unplanned events. Deal with them with the assurance that He is in control.

PRAYER – Father, I realise that You have a reason for allowing certain things to happen In my life. I ask You to give me the assurance that You will enable me to cope.

JUNE 3rd

Ephesians 4v11-13   Philippians 3v12-14   1Peter 2v1

It is so easy to envy folk who do things that look so good and are so helpful. They seem to take everything in their stride.

Do you have this feeling about certain people who seem to have so much knowledge about the Scriptures? When you look to Jesus you realise that He is so perfect and you long to be like Him. However, God knows how you are. He knows the tasks He wants you to do for Him. You watch someone, maybe singing for the Lord or preaching and you long to be able to sing or preach like that. Do not envy them. Remember, you have a specific role that God has planned for you to fulfil. Probably the other person you envy could not do your task anyhow, because that is not his gifting. Remember that and concentrate on what you have to do.

PRAYER – Father, I want to develop the gift You have given to me. Forgive me if I envy others and help me to concentrate on my own responsibilities, with Jesus' help.

JUNE 4th

Psalm 119v165   Isaiah 55v9   Philippians 4v7

To gaze over the stillness of a sheltered lake in the twilight hours brings a sense of peace and tranquillity so different to the clatter of a busy street.

Are there times when you long to find a centre of peace in the midst of a busy day? There are times as a Christian follower when you tend to be too busy. This means that you do not spend enough time in God's presence, reading and learning from His Word and listening to what He has to say. You need to stop, take time out and rest. In the long run you will be so much more effective in your work and witness. Seek the Lord while He may be found and call upon Him in the stillness.

PRAYER – Father, Your peace is so beautiful and I want to experience it in my own life. I do tend to rush about. Please help me to stop from time to time so that I may experience the loveliness of quietness, peace and tranquillity that You alone can give.

JUNE 5th

1Samuel 15v22   Luke 17v10   1Corinthians 4v7

A well trained domestic animal takes obedience in its stride, but this is only after careful instruction and schooling.

Does obedience come natural to you or do you struggle and have your own idea about things? To be a faithful witness for God, you must obey His Word in order to carry out His plan and purpose for your life. Pride just loves to take over, with self interest and every other aspect that brings glory to you. How human we all are, yet we can use all our disobediences to bring glory to His name. Have constant fellowship with Jesus so that human pride does not have a chance to master you. To be obedient you need to be trained and instructed. Jesus can take care of this. Trust and obey for there is no other way, to be happy in Jesus but to trust and obey.

PRAYER – Father, forgive my disobedient nature. I want to behave and follow Your instructions, but in my weakness I do not always react in the right way, but I do trust You.

JUNE 6th

Zephaniah 3v17   Ephesians 3v17-19   1John 4v18-21

When a couple feel attracted to one another, then real love takes over and to a degree, other things are put to one side. This sort of love could be for other special things or occasions too.

Are you conscious of a special love that takes place in your life? How does it effect other activities? If you do not love Jesus with all your heart and mind, He loves you even so, but it will be impossible for His love to show in you and radiate to others. You should be so full of His love that it will just overflow. You must overflow with Him first, just as if you were loving someone here, with a genuine real love. Praise God that Jesus means so much to us.

PRAYER Father, I want my love for You to overflow and radiate and bring others into Your very presence. Praise and glory be to Jesus.

JUNE 7th

Psalm 20v4-7   Philippians 4v6   1 Thessalonians 5v17

There are occasions in life when answers just will not come to us. When we watch baby animals, we wonder how they seem to know what to do before they have even been shown. We find it hard to understand.

Do you have times when you cannot understand something or somebody and wonder why you cannot find an answer? How difficult it is to keep on praying and not to get an answer. It is so important for you to understand that God knows all about your particular prayer request and He will only permit an answer in His time, however delayed it seems to you. Time is no object to God and His timing is always perfect. You must learn to be persistent in prayer to keep you in constant touch with the Lord.

PRAYER – Father, I am so full of praise because You have everything under control. I thank you that when I pray you will answer. Just help me to be more patient.

JUNE 8th

Psalm 23v6-7   2 Corinthians 9v8   Philippians 4v19

When we enter a garden and admire the beauty of the flowers, do we realise how much the plants depend on the soil? To provide such beautiful blooms the soil needs to be rich with a variety of nutriments of the right blend for the plant. Then one can be confident that the results will be good.

It is absolutely certain that God will supply all that you need. He knows your particular requirements so there is absolutely no need for you to be anxious. He will not give you everything you ask for unless that thing is necessary or of His will. At the same time God will give you a sense of satisfaction and peace when you trust Him. He knows what you need and will see that you have what is necessary. Praise Him for all that He has provided for you and be confident that He will continue to do so.

PRAYER – Father, I thank you that You provide all that I need to grow and develop in faith. I long to bring pleasure to others and to share with them all you have done for me.

JUNE 9th

2Corinthians 10v4   Ephesians 6v10-17   1Peter 5v8-9

It is so important to be alert these days when we are driving on the road. You never know what other drivers are going to do, so you find yourself thinking for everyone.

When you start into a new day, do you protect yourself against any danger that may confront you? Satan will constantly try to attack you one way or another and you must be constantly in touch with Jesus to help you. When He is in control, His power is far stronger than Satan's power. How easy it is to let circumstances and temptations get the better of you, if you tackle these things on your own. Keep watch and pray and use the weapons of faith and power. Trust in the Lord with all your might and lean not unto your own understanding.

PRAYER – Father, only by Your power can I resist all the attacks of Satan. Give me the desire to walk in the way You have planned for me; a determination to follow Jesus.

JUNE 10th

Matthew 18v23-33   Ephesians 4v23-27   Colossians 3v12-17

There is something very encouraging and pleasing when we observe two people who have had a fierce argument, finally deciding to forgive one another.

Have you had an occasion recently when you have been ready to forgive someone, even if you may not completely agree with them? You need to be much more loving and forgiving when you face up to people who don't always agree with you. In a situation like this you may say things you regret when you are agitated. It is so easy to get upset and resentful. Keep your eyes upon Jesus and you will automatically reflect His love. Now you will find you can forget and forgive and have more concern for people you come into contact with. Always try to be helpful and kind.

PRAYER – Father, help me to consider others and not to criticise or argue with their thoughts and ideas. This is not my responsibility. Forgive me, Lord, and make me more loving and kind.

JUNE 11th

Psalm 103v11-14   Proverbs 3v5-6   2 John 6

At the end of World War 2, on victory day, the King and Queen came on to the balcony at Buckingham Palace. Crowds came down the Mall and cheered as they gathered round the Palace gates.

Do you like to join the crowd to honour the Lord? Remember that God is always beside you watching everything you do and knowing everything you think. Do you acknowledge Him as you should? He is so gentle and understanding. Jesus is in control as you hand your life over to Him. Then you will want to be in constant touch with the King of Kings, and rejoice with the crowds as He reveals Himself to you.

PRAYER – Father, I want to honour and obey You and let the Spirit in my heart work out the purposes for my life. Please help me by Your grace and mercy.

JUNE 12th

Psalm 66v8-12   Philippians 3v12-14   Colossians 3v1-4

Edmund Hillary conquered Mt Everest. It was a long climb and he had to face many difficulties along the way. But he pressed on and overcame the difficulties and conquered.

No doubt there have been times when you have come against problems as you have aimed for a certain goal. Is this so? Unless you go through times of testing and trial, you cannot be adequately prepared for the real life ahead that God has planned for you. As we have considered so often, this life is just a training place and Jesus is in command. Learn to endure all that He wants to teach you. If you consider the tests too hard, remember He promised to only take you to a limit that you could bear.

PRAYER – Father, it is not always easy to follow where You lead, but I thank you that as I endure in Your strength, I will be able to reach the final goal. Thank you Lord.

JUNE 13th

Psalm 40v8   Romans 7v18-25   1John 2v6

When rescuers are struggling to find people after a building has collapsed, they do not stop digging until they have found every buried body. They persist.

Do you persist in your search for the truths of God through His Word and through prayer? However much you love Jesus, you still have to cope with human ways which will always be a burden. But you can rise above your human failures and disappointments by trusting Jesus to 'take over.' You will still be confronted by these things but when you commit them to Jesus, He will transform them into experiences which will build you up. Then your life will be changed into His likeness. Live a life of praise and thanksgiving and persist in following the way of truth.

PRAYER – Father, I do desire to do Your will and pray that as I persist to do so, You will encourage me through the guidance of Jesus in my life.

JUNE 14th

John 15v20-21   1Corinthians 1v3-7   1Peter 4v12-16

On the whole the older generation do not find this modern world of technology easy to understand. One is humiliated by computers, when one confers with youngsters who seem to know just how they operate and find delight in showing off their skills to the older folk.

Do you sometimes have a humiliating experience in your Christian life? Suffering for Christ can mean more than physical suffering. You may be misunderstood or you may be ridiculed but all these experiences are really meant for good. They help you to become more conscious of Jesus and your need for Him. If you try to cope with these things on your own, you may get discouraged. Hold nothing back from Jesus. He knows what it is to be humiliated and He will give you the ability to accept it too.

PRAYER - Father, I do not feel comfortable when people humiliate me, but I thank you that You sent Jesus so that He would understand and help me to stand up to something with which He was familiar whilst here on earth.

JUNE 15th

       1Timothy 6v17-19   1Peter 5v2-4   1John 5v14-15

The sheepdog has a lot more to do if the flock of sheep refuse to go where he drives them. It is much easier if the sheep are willing to co-operate.

When you are in the middle of a particularly busy project, have you been willing to stop when something or someone has suddenly appeared to interrupt your programme? To follow Jesus you must be willing to commit everything to Him in all sincerity, willing to let Him have your life in every detail. Only when you reach this point can He plead with the Father. Then your life can be moulded as He planned and it will be possible for His glory to radiate from your life in joy, praise and thanksgiving.

PRAYER – Father, please help me to be more willing to serve You in dedicating my life completely. Make me willing to help so many who need to understand and love You.

JUNE 16th

       2Corinthians 1v12   Colossians 4v5-6   1Peter 3v15-17

Animal life can teach us something about having a conscience. Mothers, wild or tame, devote their time to their off-springs, caring, feeding and warding off danger.

Are you conscientious about your ministry for Jesus and do you look for every opportunity to witness for Him? You should be so involved with Jesus that you want to share His love with others all the time, in every situation. It is not necessary to 'preach' to folks, but be conscious about your general approach, what you do and how you do it; your attitude of love and concern. We all have different gifts in our ministry. Keep to the gifting that God has blessed you with. Trust the Lord in every situation and let Him have His way.

PRAYER – Father, I am so conscious of my need to be more faithful in Your service. Help me to get my priorities right and always be conscious of the needs of others and of their need of You.

JUNE 17th

Psalm 62v5-8   Isaiah 30v15   Matthew 11v28

When it comes to holiday time we breathe a sigh of relief. At last we are able to relax away from the busy rush of 'living.'

How often do you really relax? Can you just sit back and let the world go by? What a tremendous thought to know that God has all your plans and arrangements worked out. Relax in the Lord and let the Holy Spirit take over. Deal with one situation at a time and be constantly in prayer so that you keep in close contact with God. Jesus knows what God wants for you, so He will put those desires within you. Rest, therefore, in the Lord and relax in His love.

PRAYER – Father, I praise You that You have made time possible for me to stop for rest and relaxation in Your love. With the strength and refreshment I receive, may I encourage others to do the same.

JUNE 18th

Ephesians 2v18   Hebrews 10v19-22   Hebrews 4v16

It is so interesting to notice how nature is full of obedience. Everything seems to happen when it should. The seasons change from spring through to winter. Animals and plants respond accordingly in obedience.

Do you always obey what you know is the right thing to do? It is wonderful that you can come into close contact with God through Jesus. He opened the way because He was willing to obey His Father, and you too can get into direct contact with God. However, you must be obedient to the Spirit as you are guided, directed and called. Let go and let God use you as He desires. In obedience, you will have faith to believe that it is possible for you to come into the very presence of God.

PRAYER – Father, I am not always obedient in what I do and think. Please help me to understand how necessary it is for me to have complete trust in Jesus. I know that He is able to bring me close to You in complete surrender and faithful obedience.

JUNE 19th

Proverbs 19v20-21   Ephesians 4v21-24   1Peter 1v13-16

Looking back over the years, we realise that we learnt to accept what parents and teachers taught us, as the natural and normal way of doing and saying things.

Today, are you able to accept the modern way of things; behaviour, customs etc? They are so different in so many ways. Life is a constant battle and you must be prepared to face up to this fact as a Christian, because it is all part of your training programme for a wonderful life to come. You will receive strength and knowledge through such experiences which now seem to be such a trial and a burden. Consider your reactions and accept the fact that Jesus is your Teacher, God is your Father and they want the best for you.

PRAYER – Father, There are so many things that I need to know and accept as you seek to teach me the way I should go and how I need to listen to You day by day. Thank you, Lord, for Your patience and concern.

JUNE 20th

Matthew 6v33-34   Hebrews 13v8   James 4v14-15

When the day is full of various activities it is no good thinking about more activities or appointments etc, that are going to happen tomorrow. There are only 24 hours in a day and a considerable number of those will be spent sleeping anyhow!

How many times do you try to fit 3 days into one? It is so important just to concentrate on today. Whatever happened yesterday or before is finished and can be forgotten. You can only hope that time past has been used correctly. If there were mistakes there is nothing you can do about it now, so you may as well cast it from your mind. You can be assured that the Lord will take care of tomorrow and you can sort out the details with Him when you get there. Today is your concern, one hour at a time, watching your Leader for directions and guidance.

PRAYER – Father, when my days seem so full, please help me to sort things out and get them in the right order. Then I can be guided by You and calmly tackle every task peacefully.

JUNE 21st

Luke 3v11   Ephesians 4v29-32   1John 2v3-6

There are a large number of charity organisations operating relief programmes these days. What a joy they bring to many refugee and disaster areas as they share so much that many have contributed to help them.

Do you have a feeling of great happiness when you share good things with others? It is very necessary to keep a constant check on your attitude to others. Human nature is constantly at war with the Spirit so it is essential to keep close to Jesus so that your nature reveals a Christ like attitude to consider the needs of others. It is your privileged responsibility to share His love in every situation.

PRAYER – Father, there are so many people in spiritual need and I want to share all that I have found in Jesus. Please enable me to do Your will in this and I will experience great joy and satisfaction.

JUNE 22nd

2 Corinthians 5v14-15   Colossians 3v3-4   1John 4v19-21

There are so many imitations in life today; replicas of antique furniture and likeness models representing a host of things. They are similar to the real thing but not the same.

Have you ever been drawn into a situation where you have considered something to be genuine and then found that it is just a copy of the real thing? The Christian life can be like this. There are folks who consider that if they are linked with a church, go on occasions, read the Bible and pray from time to time, they are now genuine Christians. The Christian life means more than this. Let your thoughts and life be so concentrated on Jesus and the Word of God, then the things of life will grow strangely dim in the light of His glorious love.

PRAYER Father, I want to know that my love for Jesus far outweighs my love for all the pleasures this world offers. Please help me to be faithful.

JUNE 23rd

Isaiah 61v1   Romans 8v26-27   Ephesians 6v17-18

Electric lights can look very attractive with elaborate shades and interesting fixtures. But until the electricity is switched on, there will be no light coming forth.

Are there times when you feel right, but don't seem to know how to pray? Without the work and presence of the Holy Spirit in your life, you will never be able to communicate freely with the Father. When things are rough and difficult for you to understand, you have to realise that this is all in God's plan and purpose. Everything may look very nice but you must have the power of the Spirit in your life for the light to shine.

PRAYER – Father, I rejoice in the privilege of Your Spirit in my life and I desire to share my faith with others who have needs and those who need Jesus in their life.

JUNE 24th

Matthew 6v25-34   Philippians 4v4-7   James 4v14-15

In countries where wild animals wander, it is necessary for farmers to secure domestic animals in a safe enclosure during the night. They are not concerned about the next day and are thankful that the animals came to no harm the day before.

Are you anxious about all the activities of tomorrow? It is very necessary for you not to worry. Put a fence round today and concentrate on all within that boundary. Then you can relax and know that you are safe because Jesus is in that boundary too. He will provide all you need for one day and will prepare you for tomorrow. Place yourself in His hands and let Him guide you through the programme of the day, calmly and at peace. No room for panic in a confined space. Yesterday is past; tomorrow is still to come.

PRAYER – Father, I find it so easy to get worried when I consider all I have to do each day. Thank you that you shelter me from danger in the presence of Jesus.

JUNE 25th

1Corinthians 13v10-12   Ephesians 5v8-14   Colossians 1v15-18

How lovely it is to look out over a magnificent view of distant hills and valleys, to see the animals grazing peacefully in the fields and the sun shining through the trees.

Is there a particular view that you remember; a view that brings joy as a memory of the past? As you gaze across a memory you see so much detail, but now it is obscured because the 'weather' is misty and dull. This is how it is with Jesus sometimes. One day all will be clear, then another day the distance is blurred and there is no detail to depict. Your life is like this, but one day all will be clear and that will be a wonderful day indeed. So knowing there is clarity beyond the mist, carry on and praise the Lord in anticipation. It's not easy but you must just trust and obey.

PRAYER – Father, please help me to see where I am going as I gaze over the way before me. Thank you that You assure me that the mist will clear as I put my trust in You.

JUNE 26th

Psalm 6v9   Psalm 65v2-5   1Peter 3v12

When a world disaster occurs or other tragedies, they take precedence in the world news. Suddenly the media remembers that there is a God and they turn to prayer.

Do you wait for a problem to trouble you before you turn to God in prayer? You may turn to God and plead for certain things, but you must be sincere when you pray. Pray in depth and understanding, not only when you have a desperate need, but always, every day, bringing praise and thanksgiving into your prayers. You cannot see God or Jesus, but you can have close communion with them. Believe that Jesus is always waiting to listen and to plead with the Father on your behalf.

PRAYER – Father, when everything seems to be going well, I tend to take it all for granted. Forgive me when I neglect my time of prayer and fellowship with You.

JUNE 27th

Job 22v21   John 14v27   Romans 5v1-2

A beautiful garden creates peace. The birds are singing, a stream flows and a gentle breeze rustles the leaves in the trees. What a wonderful feeling of relaxation and peace.

Are there special times when you are conscious of God's peace in your life? How we all long for the peace of God to saturate our lives to such an extent that we are constantly relaxed and at ease. This is the way you need to be sure that the Holy Spirit can take over completely and just use you as He wants, to the glory of God. Just rest peacefully in His love. This attitude is infectious and you can radiate love and peace to those with whom you come into contact, so that they will know love and peace too.

PRAYER – Father, I long for the true peace that You alone can give me. As I relax and bathe in Your love, help me to pass on to others all that Your peace means to me.

JUNE 28th

Psalm 32v7   Ephesians 6v10-18   2 Thessalonians 3v1-5

Men working on a building project wear steel helmets. This is a protection against a fall or against part of the construction falling on them.

Do you put on the armour of protection against the enemy each day? It is necessary for you to put on the protection of Jesus day by day. You are told about this in Scripture and you need to be aware. Satan is constantly on the attack and you do not know when, so you must be protected against him. You need to be very sensitive to Jesus' guidance and always listening. The Word of God is your light and you will receive your instructions by constant study of it each day.

PRAYER – Father, thank you that I am protected by You, from Satan and all his unsavoury ways. With the shield of protection and faith, I go forward.

JUNE 29th

Psalm 37v3-6   Proverbs 3v5-6   Romans 10v11-13

When we travel by bus or train we assume that the driver knows where he is going and that he understands his vehicle. We trust him to get us to our destination.

Do you have complete confidence in Jesus when you commit your life to Him? Do you trust Him to take you safely to your destination? It is easy for you to read in God's Word how you need to trust Jesus to lead you through life. But He cannot lead you successfully if you are always pulling in one direction or another, like a dog on a lead. Accept what Jesus says and let your life be guided by relaxing in His love. Reflect His love, trust Him and be free to praise Him with a thankful heart.

PRAYER – Father, I trust You to lead me through life and through all the events you want me to experience. Please help me to be faithful as I try to follow the pathway set before me.

JUNE 30th

Proverbs 3v11-12   Hebrews 12v4-6   Revelations 3v19-22

To watch troops marching to the rhythm of an accompanying band is a thrilling experience. To appear in such immaculate form takes much discipline. The result is very stimulating.

As each day dawns, do you discipline yourself to plan your day, and seek to follow where the Lord leads you? Unless you are corrected, you will not know that you are on the wrong course. If you fail to respond to the Lord, He will have cause to correct you, but at the same time will point out the error. As He disciplines you in this way, He will enable you to plan your daily programme. You will know that the Father loves you, otherwise He would not spend time with all this discipline, training and correcting.

PRAYER – Father, I enjoy making my own plans but as I study Your Word, I realise how necessary it is to accept YOUR plans, and to accept Your discipline. Thank you Lord, for correcting me.

JULY

JULY 1st

Psalm 51v10-11   John 14v23-27   Acts 1v7-8

Electric appliances are useless standing by themselves, and will not work if the power is not switched on; but when electric power is released, the appliance being used will operate as it should.

How often do you turn to the Lord for the necessary power He gives through His Holy Spirit? God is within you in Spirit, therefore you should reveal Him in your attitudes. When you 'switch on' to the power of the Spirit, you will be filled with joy and praise. You will then have the strength you need to do the tasks God has assigned to you. You have a duty to share this love and compassion, taking every opportunity to pass on the joy of the Lord, but you must 'switch on' first.

PRAYER – Father, I admit that I do not always think to 'switch on' so that I may receive the power of Your Spirit. I pray that when I do, I may be used to spread Your love and blessings to others.

JULY 2nd

Psalm 119v33-35   Proverbs 2v6-11   Acts 8v26-35

Life is getting so complicated these days and unless we have special training in the modern technology of so many things, we do not have the necessary knowledge to understand.

Can you handle and understand the more difficult parts of Scripture without help? How much we all need to know the Lord. This can only be done by constant communion with Him in prayer and meditation. Share everything with Him and listen to Him if you want to understand. To be with Him in Spirit is just like getting to know a friend really well, the sort of friend that you can really chat to in a relaxed way, with no tension or embarrassment. Share everything in perfect confidence and He will understand you and want you to understand Him too.

PRAYER – Father, I thank you for the wonderful peace that fills my heart when I turn to You and ask You to open my eyes as I search to understand Your Word.

JULY 3rd

Galatians 4v7   Ephesians 1v3-14   1John 3v1

Children cannot grow up on their own without parental care. They need to be taught, disciplined and cared for.

Have you ever tried to teach someone how to study the Scriptures without someone first helping you to understand? As a child of God, having been accepted into the family of God through faith in Jesus Christ, you know that He has a special care and responsibility for you. He will make sure that you have all that is good for you, and will correct and instruct you too. What a wonderful thought to know that God is your Father. He may have to correct you from time to time, but in the end you will be part of one happy family to create love, joy, peace, gentleness and understanding amongst friends and family.

PRAYER – Father, I praise and thank you that I can call You Father and know that I am really part of Your family. Thank you that You sent Jesus to teach this wonderful truth.

JULY 4th

Job 33v28-30   Romans 3v21-26   1Peter 1v13-21

When someone falls into deep water and cannot swim, what a relief it is when he is rescued by someone who is able to save him from drowning.

Are you ever in a spiritual situation where you are completely out of your depth of understanding? It is only through God's goodness in sacrificing His Son Jesus Christ. Because He suffered, you have been redeemed. God is not angry with you, because you acknowledge Jesus as Lord and try to live in obedience and love to God. However, you must be prepared for correction. God will never leave you alone when you claim Him as Father.

PRAYER – Father, I praise You that I have been redeemed from my sinful background and can now live in the freedom and love that You alone can give me in Jesus. Thank you Lord.

JULY 5th

John 3v16   Ephesians 2v4-10   1John 4v19-21

There are certain things that are more attractive to us than others. As individuals we differ in our choice of things, and what we love and enjoy, may not be the same for others.

What is your particular choice of things which you can honestly say you love? You will never fully understand God's wonderful love for you. He delights in you, but often you are slow to respond to such love. Do not get agitated or concerned when things do not always seem to go right. Remember, God has you in the hollow of His hand and will provide all that He considers necessary. He is always ready to forgive and even if He does become angry sometimes, it is only because He loves you and wants the best for you. Radiate this love in your concern for others so they too may be able to share the joy and blessings of God's love.

PRAYER – Father, Your love overwhelms me. You gave Your love by sending Jesus. May I share that love with so many who are in need.

JULY 6th

Proverbs 12v18   2 Corinthians 8v16-21   Colossians 4v2-6

The world seems to be full of disagreements and discontent these days, with continual criticisms and complaints.

How often do you complain about people who tend to differ with your Christian beliefs? How easy it is to say things in the heat of the moment that you later regret. You need to be continually on your guard that you do not upset or offend, criticise or complain. Instead, concentrate on trying to say things that will please and comfort, so bring praise to the name of Jesus. It is so necessary for you to keep 'in tune' with the Lord, so that He can reveal His love for others through you. Love is the basis of service and witness along the Christian pathway and Jesus depends on you.

PRAYER – Father, it is so easy to find fault, to criticise and disagree. Help me to be more careful, considerate and understanding, so that I can be helpful and can thus share the love of Jesus in my life.

JULY 7th

1Corinthians 10v13   2Corinthians 12v9   Hebrews 4v15-16

When an animal accidentally steps into a swamp it is in trouble. It struggles to extricate itself from the sucking mud and if not helped, is liable to give up the struggle and sink deeper.

Have you ever found yourself in difficulties that overwhelm you, so that you just want to 'give up'? You need to realise and be thankful to know that Jesus understands all the problems that surround you daily to try to pull you down. He experienced the same problem, but was so united with His Father, that these things never overcame Him. So with you, if you are one with Jesus, these weaknesses and temptations will not overcome you. You really need to be and feel absolutely weak, so that the Lord can take over. Let go and let God. His love will never fail you.

PRAYER – Father, when I get into a 'swamp' of trouble, help me in my weakness and give me faith to know that you will get me out. How wonderful to know you are there.

JULY 8th

John 1v12-13   Romans 8v12-17   1John 3v2-3

It is so lovely to watch a flock of sheep when all the little lambs begin to arrive. Every mother knows exactly which lamb belongs to her and keeps a constant watch on it.

Do you sometimes wonder which Scripture verse comes from which Book? How would you cope with the situations all around you, without the firm and certain assurance of knowing that God is your Father and takes care of you. One day you are going to be like Jesus and meet Him face to face. It is exciting to think of the future ahead, but right now you have to be in the world, constantly confronted by evil thoughts and ways. Stay near to Jesus and follow His desires. You are a child of God.

PRAYER – Father, what an honour it is to be known as a child of God; I am not worthy. Please give me the ability to recognise my responsibility to obey and serve You, my Heavenly Father.

JULY 9th

Psalm 32v1-2   Romans 7v15-25   Colossians 3v5-10

Although we cannot always see it, sin is everywhere. This is so in the plant world, and when we see a plant wither and die, aphids or mould may be the cause. These things are hidden, but they are still unpleasant and unwanted.

How often are you conscious of sin tucked away in your life, often unnoticed? Praise the Lord that Jesus has cleansed you from your sins of yesterday. But to keep that cleanliness, you need to come before the Lord each day for a fresh anointing of Holy Spirit cleansing. In so doing the hidden particles of sinful thoughts and actions that creep in unnoticed will be removed. Keep in constant communication with the Lord.

PRAYER – Father, I want to search every part of my life and clear out all the sinful thoughts or ideas that create unwanted items in my life. Please help me to stay close to Jesus and be guided by His cleansing power.

JULY 10th

Psalm 119v27-28   Philippians 4v4-7   Hebrews 12v2-6

With computers and technical equipment, it is necessary to keep up a regular practice in order to understand how it works.

Are there times when you seem to be out of touch with God? It is important to try to realise how vital it is to be in constant touch with Jesus. Each day you need His presence, especially when you get into the daily routine and you find yourself absorbed with problems. But if you have a 'rough patch' then remember, He is watching you, so you should watch Him too. In this way, you will understand Him and want to share your understanding with others. Do you realise how much Jesus relies upon your witness?

PRAYER – Father, there is so much I do not understand in the Christian walk, but thank you for Jesus Who helps me to understand all that I need to know.

JULY 11th

Isaiah 41v9-10   Hebrews 2v14-18   Hebrews 4v12-16

It is a fact that diamonds have to be severely chipped and polished before the finished product develops into a sparkling gem.

Do you get disturbed or troubled when you are experiencing times of upsetting circumstances? When you have suffered and been tempted, you are much more able to understand the sufferings of others. This is how it is with Jesus. He went through so much physical and mental suffering, that He is able to understand your suffering too. He does more than understand because He is with you to protect, encourage and strengthen you. Then He will bring peace and comfort when you begin to find the burdens too hard to bear.

PRAYER – Father, despite any suffering I may experience, physical or otherwise, I praise You because Jesus is with me all the day long and will satisfy me with all I need.

JULY 12th

Exodus 33v14   Joshua 1v9   Hebrews 3v13-14

When we are introduced to a new food that we have not tried before, we tend to have doubts. Will I like the taste? Will it upset my stomach? We hesitate; we have doubts.

Are there times when you doubt what you read in Scripture? Why do you have doubts? You are a child of God; He is your Father. Surely you can trust Him to look after your every need. In the Word you will read that He has promised to do so. You should be satisfied with this. The only thing you need to deal with is your disobedience. You should have no fear of turmoil or distress around you, but go on in faith. Know that the Lord will not let you fail.

PRAYER – Father, I do tend to hesitate and doubt some things that I read in Your Word. Forgive me and fill me with the joy and certainty that You alone can provide.

JULY 13th

Romans 8v38-39   Colossians 4v2   2Timothy 1v12

In the construction of a tower, it is absolutely essential for the various parts to be constructed in the right order with no unnecessary gaps which would throw the construction out and weaken the whole structure.

When you spend time with the Lord in prayer, do you get interruptions that throw your thoughts 'out of gear?' When you keep absolutely close to God, nothing can possibly get in between. So when things begin to disturb you, such as anxiety, fear, worries etc, it means that you are not close enough and these things tend to take the place of God. To rid your thoughts of such things, you must be more diligent in prayer. Then the gap will close and unnecessary things will be squeezed out.

PRAYER – Father, I owe You so much for Your love and mercy. I want to do all that I can to give You glory and be willing for You to use me as you want to do, with no gaps in between.

JULY 14th

Luke 6v45   Ephesians 4v29-32   Colossians 4v5-6

When people disagree and allow themselves to become angry, words begin to fly and often people are hurt and embarrassed by words spoken that are not meant to be.

How easy it is to say things and then regret what you have said. If you have said something in the 'heat of the moment' that is out of place, then that thought must have been in your heart in the first place, or you would not have said it. Have you ever been in this sort of situation? Oh! How important it is to lay your heart open before God each day, that He may cleanse it and fill it with His Spirit. Then you will want to be a blessing to people and desire to help and love them. If your heart is right with God, then you will be able to do just that.

PRAYER – Father, forgive me for the unkind thoughts I sometimes have about someone. Help me to be more loving and thoughtful and so enable Your blessings to flow.

JULY 15th

Matthew 7v15-23   Mark 4v21-25   1Thessalonians 5v19-24

A visit to the waxworks centre in London is an amazing experience. Apart from the fact that no figure is moving, it is very difficult to realise that this is not the real person before you.

It is so easy to believe all that people say is true, but you need to remember that this is not always so. When it comes to spiritual issues, the Word of God is truth, and you must be convinced that instructions and teachings found here come only through God speaking. Do you believe all that you read in Scripture? When you have this principle right the Lord will refresh and strengthen you. Obey the Lord, do what He says, go where He sends you and ignore false suggestions and ideas so often put before you. Trust wholly in the Lord alone.

PRAYER – Father, may I always take Your Word as the only true way to live my Christian life. Give me a willing heart to listen with wise discernment.

JULY 16th

Matthew 26v41   Luke 10v17-20   1Peter 5v6-11

If you happen to wander into an attractive pasture which, unbeknown to you, is occupied by a giant bull, it is likely that he will have something to say. You will hastily depart before he overtakes you, I'm sure!

The very presence of Satan in the world today is real and you will be constantly seeking to overcome him. This you cannot do in your own strength, but must be continually conscious of God's presence. You need to pray constantly that Jesus will protect you from the power of Satan. Jesus will help you to discern His leading and not to be misguided by satanic urges. Now you will be stronger in the Lord to stand up to the evil temptations of Satan and you will have power to overcome.

PRAYER – Father, I praise the name of Jesus and thank Him for His protection and His love, resulting in peace and joy in my heart.

JULY 17th

Romans 5v1-5   1 Corinthians 12v1-11   Ephesians 5v8-14

Milk heated up suddenly reaches a point when it will overflow because of a hidden power that forces it to a point of expansion.

When you let God's love flood your heart, it is bound to overflow to others and this is what He wants. This really pleases Him. But it means that you must 'roll away the stone' and uncover any fault or sin or unkind thought. Reveal these things to the Lord and ask His forgiveness and mercy. Then when He has cleansed these things away, He can fill you with His Spirit. Now His light, love, peace and joy will be revealed in the abilities He gives you to serve Him.

PRAYER – Father, thank you for Your overflowing love and mercy. I praise You and pray that this love may overflow to others who need Your presence in their lives.

JULY 18th

2 Samuel 22v31-37   Psalm 32v8-10   John 14v6

On a long car journey a good map is essential and if the driver has someone to read the map and navigate, then this is even better.

The Lord has your way all mapped out. All you need to do is to be constantly in tune with Him, to make sure you are 'on course.' When you lose contact you are likely to go 'off course.' Follow Jesus and keep in touch with Him constantly. The road may be steep in places, in other parts you may need to use the brakes to slow down a bit, but always keep in tune with your Guide and He will direct your way.

PRAYER – Father, thank you that Jesus is always by my side to 'keep me going.' Help me to listen to His directions that will prevent me from taking the wrong road.

JULY 19th

Exodus 15v13   Proverbs 4v10-12   Hebrews 13v17

The army officer is in complete control of his company. He leads the men forth in an orderly fashion and they follow his commands, instructions and movements. This results in perfect unity. Any false step is quickly noticed and corrected.

God is in complete control of all our lives. Do you respond to His commands? He is God above all other gods. You should be humbled to think that He even takes trouble and care over you; one amongst so many. You tend to get frustrated and try to sort things out on your own, while all the time He has the whole of your way organised to the last detail. One day you will see the tapestry taking shape.

PRAYER – Father, I marvel that You go before me in full control. Help me to listen to Your commands and obediently follow where You lead.

JULY 20th

Nehemiah 8v10   Habakkuk 3v17-19   Romans 5v1-5

Witnessing a football game either in person or on television, displays an air of explosive excitement when a goal is scored. Everyone is filled with joy.

However much you are surrounded by trials and sorrows, you need not be 'cast down,' instead rejoice in the Lord. You should be radiant as you participate in the Christian life and let the light of Jesus shine forth to all, helping and encouraging them with praise. This inner joy will enable you to be strong and prepared to tackle great things for the Lord.

PRAYER – Father, I want to be an encourager and I know this will mean adopting an attitude of joy in my heart that will radiate from me to those who need Your love.

JULY 21st

Psalm 25v4-5   Proverbs 21v30   Isaiah 58v11

Designs, ideas and inspirations seen today are modern and often stark. The older generations find it difficult to accept these modern trends but they have to accept that this is the way things are today.

It is so easy for you to get ideas and inspirations which you feel are good and right, but it is so important to be absolutely certain that God is guiding these ideas. Satan is very much alive and delights to intervene. You must pray that you will be able to discern and only move in the direction that the Lord prepares for you. Daily seek the cleansing power of the Lord, through the Holy Spirit and only follow His Way.

PRAYER – Father, I am so good in making my own arrangements according to my own ideas. Please help me to seek your will and purpose for my arrangements and keep faithful.

JULY 22nd

2 Chronicles 7v14   Matthew 6v5-8   John 15v9-17

When there is a crisis in the land, the whole country turns to special days of prayer. People turn to God in such a way when they have crises in their own lives. Otherwise, God is just around but on the whole, people do not seem to spend much time in His presence.

If you become anxious or in pain, do you turn more frequently to Jesus? You should really want to turn to Him all the time, but it is so easy to become absorbed in the work of the day, that you tend to forget. But Jesus is always beside you and His love will always protect you. What ever situation you are in, pray continually with grateful thanks. Through the gentleness of the Holy Spirit, your situation will be dealt with and you will be encouraged and helped.

PRAYER – Father, I pray that the love of Jesus will radiate from my life as I draw closer to You. Your love will not let me go, but will be shared with those in need.

JULY 23rd

Romans 8v6-8   Ephesians 6v18   1 Thessalonians 5v17

Workers in the airport control tower need to be in constant touch with the planes. At the same time, pilots in the planes need to be in constant touch with the airport control tower. Otherwise there could be a disaster.

It is not enough just to casually meet with Jesus, commit the day to Him and then forget Him until the evening. You need to be in constant touch with the 'control tower' throughout the day. Remember, that Jesus is constantly in touch with you and if you do not respond, disaster could happen. Are you alert for any signs of Satan getting into your life in some subtle way? You need urgent guidance from the 'control tower.'

PRAYER – Father, I thank you that Jesus is continually ready to guide me in the right route. Please help me to keep in constant touch.

JULY 24th

Matthew 4v10-11   Romans 12v1-8   1Peter 4v10-11

Waiters have to learn the correct way to serve meals. They must be shown how to lay tables, how to present a meal and all the necessary technique involved.

When you belong to the Lord, you are continually having to learn how to respect and serve Him, subject to correction where necessary. As you realise this, you must remember to stand fast in the faith, believing and willing to be a good and faithful servant of the Lord. It is not easy, but has to be like this. How do you react to your training? Do not hesitate when He corrects you, but always be willing to respond. If you want to help others, you must be able to know what you are doing.

PRAYER – Father, I want to be a good steward so that I can serve and wait upon others in their spiritual needs. I will accept training and correction according to Your will and purpose for my life.

JULY 25th

Psalm 118v6-9   2Corinthians 12v10   Ephesians 6v10-18

There are so many distressing reports today, of elderly people, and also young children, who are apparently safe in their own homes behind locked doors. Then, quite unexpectedly, they are attacked by some unforeseen outsider.

How easy it is to be so confident that your life is safe in the Lord. Of course this is true; do you believe it? But at times you will be conscious of the evil one and feel the power of satanic forces around you, trying to weaken your faith. You need to be committed to Jesus, confident of the power of the Holy Spirit in your life and absolutely certain that evil powers cannot penetrate the innermost part of your life.

PRAYER – Father, as I enter into Your presence in the power of prayer, and as I study Your Word, please give me the confidence I need to put my trust in Your safe hands.

JULY 26th

Psalm 32v8-11   Isaiah 48v17   John 14v1-4

On a country ramble along unknown paths, one depends upon a map or someone who knows the way to guide you along the correct path.

There is only one straight path for you to follow and you must not attempt any other. This path involves being obedient and to go in the direction that Jesus indicates. Have you sought help and guidance about the way you should follow? Having received help yourself, now show help and love to others walking with you. You are all heading for your eternal home and the experiences you have along the way are all part of the journey. The Lord will guide you if you constantly listen to what He is saying to you.

PRAYER – Father, I want to follow Jesus, my Leader and Guide, and be a help to others who are not finding the way easy. Thank you that we know our destination and thank you that Jesus will direct us.

JULY 27th

Psalm 5v11-12   Colossians 1v13   2 Thessalonians 3v3

When someone is seen to be in great trouble or difficulty and obviously needing help, they will not be left to suffer alone. Help will come from medical or police or even a person passing by.

Are you covered by the 'cloak' of Jesus' love and protection? If you belong to Him, He has promised never to leave you. Therefore, you can know that whatever circumstances or experiences you have, Jesus is protecting you with His 'cloak.' You can always be sure too, that He will guard you against all satanic attacks. If you are enveloped in the love and security of Jesus, Satan cannot possibly penetrate that 'cloak' of protection. Trust the Lord at all times; He never makes false statements or promises.

PRAYER – Father, thank you for Jesus who protects me with His 'cloak' of love when I am in trouble. I am so grateful.

JULY 28th

John 13v34-35   Ephesians 5v1-2   1John 3v11-14

In the world of music there are certain styles we enjoy more than others and some particular pieces we just love and cannot hear them often enough.

Love undertakes for every feeling you may have about anyone or anything if you will let it. Do you notice how real love shows and cannot be hidden? Your concern for others should be such that they are always on your mind and you will be constantly praying for them, just as Jesus is constantly remembering you and all men everywhere. You need to be sensitive to your responsibility to pray for those who Jesus places on your mind to love.

PRAYER – Father, give me a heart to love and be faithful in prayer as I remember others in love before you. May they be conscious of Your love for them too.

JULY 29th

Psalm 37v3-5   Proverbs 3v5-7   Romans 10v11

When it is necessary to visit the doctor with a medical problem, it is also necessary to accept what he has to say, and accept the treatment and necessary medication he advises. We trust his judgement.

Do you trust the Lord and take His advise? How important it is to really trust the Lord. It is easy to say you trust Him, but another thing to actually mean you trust Him, letting Him take over completely with no doubts at all. Then He can do things and reveal to you that He means what He says. But He cannot prove Himself until you give yourself over to Him completely. Then you will really see Him at work, giving you freedom, release and strength.

PRAYER – Father, it is easy for me to have doubts in my mind instead of trusting in You. Help me to accept what You tell me in Your Word and to respond accordingly.

JULY 30th

Galatians 5v22-25   James 1v12-14   1Peter 5v8-9

It is very easy to be led astray by temptation when, for instance, the glossy magazine announcing a selection of sea cruises and exotic holidays, arrives in the post. But they are, in general, too expensive!

There are many temptations in the Christian life. These are all opportunities for you to grow in the character of Jesus. Do you envisage a life of love, joy, peace and self control? This kind of character takes time to develop. You will almost certainly face temptations and problems along the way and must be wise in your decisions. Remember, Satan always goes for the weakest areas in your life. He is continually poised to pounce and you need to stay continually alert.

PRAYER – Father, I ask for Your help to keep me always on the look out for trouble as I seek to draw near and become more like Jesus. I thank you for the temptations that will strengthen my faith and trust in You.

JULY 31st

Romans 5v1-5   1Peter 4v12-17   1Peter 5v10-11

Suffering a straightforward surgical operation, there is bound to be a certain amount of pain and discomfort. But as time advances, the suffering becomes less and the operation proves a success to cure the ailment.

Suffering and tribulation in the Christian life are all part of your training for the eternal life to come. You must accept this fact, counting it an honour to be chosen for such a training. Satan would like to see you sink under pressure, but Jesus is Lord of the situation and will protect, strengthen and cure you. The ministry of Holy Spirit power in your life will enable you to be victorious, strong and full of joy, also it will enable you to understand people in an acceptable way. Do you have a longing to share the love of Jesus?

PRAYER – Father, I do not enjoy suffering but realise the need to suffer from time to time. May I stay faithful and loving as I accept this suffering as part of my training

AUGUST

AUGUST 1st

Lamentations 3v22-23   Hebrews 11v6   James 5v11

Driving on a wet day, the car windscreen soon mists over and we find it difficult to see the way. It is necessary to continually wipe it as we go along.

It is vital for you to have a complete faith and dependence upon God. It is not always easy because you tend to become doubtful when circumstances appear difficult. Do you sometimes find it difficult to see clearly the way ahead? Put your hand into God's hand and have complete trust that He will lead you in the right direction. A blind man would not doubt a guide leading him across a busy road so why should you doubt the Lord, as He leads you through a busy world? Trust Him.

PRAYER – Father, I know that You will lead me across the busiest and most dangerous thoroughfare so please help me to know that I have nothing to fear.

AUGUST 2nd

Isaiah 59v16   Ephesians 2v18-19   1Peter 4v12-13 and v19

When an animal suffers or is in pain, it cannot tell us, but somehow we know and will do all we can to relieve the suffering and show it love and care.

However much suffering and anxiety you have to endure, do you always believe that God understands even if you say nothing? He knows all the details and has a purpose for every situation and circumstance. Your responsibility is to be faithful and have complete trust in Him. God sends Jesus to be specially near to you in times of stress and strain. He takes care of every situation. So you should be stronger, never doubting that Jesus is Lord and always ready to relieve your suffering and to bring you His love.

PRAYER – Father, I may not always say when I feel troubled in my faith and love for You, but I thank you that Jesus is always ready to deal with my weakness and encourage me.

AUGUST 3rd

Psalm 145v17-19   Isaiah 41v10   Hebrews 13v6-7

In a disaster situation when people may be trapped under rubble, there will be rescuers carefully listening for any sound which would indicate signs of life.

What do you do when things seem to get on top of you? The Lord is constantly listening for your cries for help. He will not delay in giving comfort, strength and love. But you must be responsive and never slow in calling for His help. In this attitude you will be heard and obstacles will be removed to release you from your suffering. As you 'surface' you will be so relieved and thankful; a time for rejoicing.

PRAYER – Father, I have been under so much pressure and discomfort, but You sent Jesus to release me in my time of need. I have responded and now I am free. Thank you for Your loving care.

AUGUST 4th

Job 23v10   Psalm 26v2-3   James 1v12

During the past few years so many new cars have been produced. Before any of these cars come on to the road, they all have to be put through a strict time of testing. This is essential.

Trials and times of testing will come to you in your Christian life. Are you ready for these? Do not let them drag you down; there will always be Jesus to see you through. He is continually watching you and is ready to rescue you when you have reached the limit of tolerance. It is very necessary for you to realise how important it is for you to be tested and prepared before starting into any service for the Lord. You need His power to strengthen you before you are ready to 'take to the open road.'

PRAYER – Father, as You 'test' me for Your service, please give me a strong and willing heart which will make me more useful in Your service.

AUGUST 5th

Jeremiah 10v23   Romans 8v26-28   Romans 12v2

There are so many places of interest to visit, but without a guide it is possible to miss a great deal of interesting detail. We trust the Guide to tell us the true facts.

You need no other Guide on your Christian journey, but Jesus. No one else can explain the land marks in such detail. Follow where He leads, living a life acceptable to Him. Then you will be sure of complete satisfaction in what you are seeing and doing. Do you relax and listen to what the Lord has to say, allowing His Spirit to take over in your life? You will learn so much more if you listen to your 'Guide' and read God's Word.

PRAYER – Father, I am so glad that Jesus is my Guide. Without His help I will miss so much. May I always keep close to Him.

AUGUST 6th

Proverbs 3v12   Jeremiah 29v11   1Peter 5v6

In all walks of life, training is so essential and we need to follow so carefully the instructions and corrections we are given and concentrate on what we have been taught.

Correction is an essential part of training. If you take no notice of God's corrections, then you will not be very fruitful. Do you sometimes feel the need for some encouragement in your life? You may think that God is not listening when you call to Him, but He is. Then, after the correction, you begin to see a pattern emerging. Your task for the Lord will be enriched and you will want to praise your wise and knowledgeable 'Trainer.'

PRAYER – Father, I am humbled when I realise how ungrateful I have been. I thank you so much that correction has lifted me up and now I have no fear Jesus will correct any faults that disturb the growth of my Christian life.

AUGUST 7th

Luke 11v9-10   John 16v23   James 4v2-3

There are times when we send for a certain item seen in a catalogue which we would like to buy. Time passes and no item arrives. We become agitated; where is your order?

No doubt you tend to get frustrated when you think that God has ignored your requests. But God never ignores any request. Have you ever asked if that request is good for you? The answer will come, because you have asked in the name of Jesus. It may not necessarily come in the way you had thought or even planned, but God knows what is best for your life and you must be prepared to accept His decisions. Be patient.

PRAYER – Father, I realise that sometimes my requests need to have the right answers and You know what the right answer should be. Thank you, that in time I will know too. Please help me to be patient.

AUGUST 8th

Romans 10v9-11   James 5v16   1John 1v8-10

When an inspection is to be made in an industrial complex, it is essential that everything is on show, and no items, however small, should be kept out of sight. This is most important for future programmes.

It is very necessary for you to have an open heart before God; nothing must be hid. You will need a daily cleansing, ridding yourself of any unhealthy thoughts or actions. Do you try to confess any unwholesome thoughts or deeds so that the Lord can really fill you to overflowing with His love, joy and peace? It is easy to hold back something; unkind thoughts, criticism, pride, envy or self pity. All these things need to be brought to the Lord. Draw near to God and He will draw near to you.

PRAYER – Father, I confess that there are hidden areas in my life that I need to share with You. Please cleanse me and set me free.

AUGUST 9th

Romans 7v14-25   Philippians 4v13   Colossians 2v6

When we are asked to get involved in some work programme that is a grade above our usual run of work, we tend to hesitate and consider that perhaps we are not worthy of such a promotion.

Is there a time when you feel unworthy of all the Lord has asked you to do for Him? There will be many times when you are disobedient and hesitant, often doubting the ways and purposes of the Lord. Why do you complain and seek self pity when you are punished? You need to learn obedience if you want to be a shining light for Jesus. Yes, it's a constant battle, but the answer is really very simple. You must spend time with the Lord and remember that Jesus is always beside you, so you just keep in step with Him and you will fit into what is required of you.

PRAYER – Father, yes I do feel unworthy for the special work You ask me to do. But with Jesus by my side, I will go forward to carry out that special task.

AUGUST 10th

Deuteronomy 4v9   Isaiah 48v17   Philippians 2v13-16

As we grow and develop, the time comes when we have to decide what to do with our life. When we finally become involved in a particular career or profession, suddenly we realise that we are in a position of responsibility, which we must faithfully recognise.

As a child of God you have a responsibility. Would you let your parents down by undesirable behaviour? God, in Jesus, sets you an example and when you look into the details of His life on earth, you see so much that you are not practicing in your own life. God has promised you so much; you must abide in Him and show forth His love and resist temptation. He will never let you down and you must never let Him down either.

PRAYER – Father, You teach me so much and I regret that I do not always do the things that You ask me to do. Please give me the desire to follow You more closely, and obediently carry out your desires for me.

AUGUST 11th

Psalm 119v49-50   Romans 4v18-21   2Peter 3v9

When we commit ourselves to something such as scouts or guides, church membership or marriage, we make promises. It is up to our faithful obedience to carry out that promise.

The Lord never breaks a promise. Then why do you doubt or get frustrated when, on reading His Word, He places before you so many promises? You have no cause for fear or anxiety when you trust in God. His promises should be a light in your life, so let this light shine through you to others, so that they too may receive His promise through Jesus Christ the Lord.

PRAYER – Father, let Your light shine through Your promises, and forgive me for my doubts. I rejoice in Your precious Word which reveals so many wonderful promises to me.

AUGUST 12th

Lamentations 3v31-32   Jeremiah 46v28   Matthew 6v33-34

When we look forward to something very special either in kind or a special event, we get excited. Then for some reason it all falls through and does not happen. What a disappointment!

Sorrow, disappointment, anxiety and fear are all part of the human makeup. But in Jesus, you can overcome these things and know that this is only part of your training programme. There are moments when God seems distant, but His love is so great towards you, that He will only leave you in this state long enough for you to realise how much you need His help and guidance. Patience is one of the hardest lessons but it has to be learnt.

PRAYER – Father, through the power of Your Spirit I will be conscious of Your strength and love when I face disappointments in life.

AUGUST 13th

1 Chronicles 28v9-10   Isaiah 55v8-9   Jeremiah 32v17-20

How exciting it is when we have a great idea and spend time planning something special with some experienced help. There will be research to do, but eventually we are confronted with the finished product, which gives us a wonderful feeling of satisfaction.

If you try to plan something, do you think you can rely on your own ideas alone? The Lord will guide you if you ask Him, but you will never know how He is going to act. You must be ready for the most unexpected things to happen. Sometimes the Lord may reveal that your ideas are not right. Listen to Him, be patient and conduct your plans so that they are in tune with the Lord.

PRAYER – Father, I sometimes get over excited about my ideas and plans. Please help me to relax and listen to the way You want my plans to be organised, so that they may bring glory to You.

AUGUST 14th

Psalm 29v11   Psalm 119v165   Isaiah 55v12

Following the busy preparation for a holiday, what a joy it is to arrive at your destination. To sit in a quiet garden or rest by the sea. It may be just in a quiet country setting. What peace.

Concentrate on joy and peace today. You really do need both of these gifts. Satan will be constantly trying to destroy your joy and peace but you must just claim Jesus as Victor every day. Do you do this despite what is going on? Have you experienced that wonderful inner peace which no one can destroy? If so, you will feel relaxed so that the moment things seem to overwhelm or upset you, inner peace will make you feel calm. Do not let problems fill you with self pity, but consider how so many in Scripture reacted when joy came into their lives. Joy and peace make a solid foundation.

PRAYER – Father, fill me with Your wonderful peace so that I can face any difficult patches in my life calmly, with joyful thanks for Your perfect guidance.

AUGUST 15th

Psalm 23v1-3   Romans 12v2   Philippians 2v12-13

Generally, when a child is corrected and told not to do a certain thing, he or she considers it is more fun to do the thing that is considered to be wrong, rather than do what they are told is right. A natural reaction, it seems!

You can only do good things when your eyes are fixed on Jesus. How often have you continued to do something you have been advised not to do? It is not normally natural to do good, because, going back to the days of Adam and Eve, basically we are all evil, living in an evil world. It is only through God's mercy you can be good. In obedience, you find joy and peace as the Holy Spirit fills your life and penetrates your whole being with love.

PRAYER – Father, I realise how easy it is to ignore goodness, but I want to bring honour and praise to You, by being like Christ in all I say and do.

AUGUST 16th

1 Corinthians 6v19-20   Ephesians 2v19-22   1Peter 2v5-6

Once the foundation of a building is complete, then the brick building can commence. These must be perfect in structure and shape etc and must fit alongside one another in harmony. The completed structure depends on the accuracy of the brickwork.

What a tremendous thought it is to consider that you are part of the building of the Church of God. Do you realise how important your contribution can be? You are a 'brick' and God chooses His 'bricks' carefully. They must be as perfect as possible and a credit to the Builder. They all fit on to the Corner Stone which is Jesus Christ. They must all 'match up' as we work as Christians together. Faulty 'bricks' will need to be corrected.

PRAYER – Father, it is such a privilege to be part of Your building programme. I do not want to be a faulty 'brick' so please correct me. I appreciate the need for me to 'fit in' to the Building.

AUGUST 17th

Galatians 6v2   Hebrews 10v24   James 5v16

Doctors and nurses have a demanding responsibility to look after their patients. They prescribe appropriate medication and treatment and have concern for the recovery of their patients.

Are you concerned about your friends and family; their welfare, their health, their outlook? It is our responsibility to be concerned about the affairs of others and to constantly uphold them in prayer. It is easy to criticise people behind their backs, but much more difficult to tell them about your criticism. Be honest and open and remember Whose you are and Whom you serve. What does Jesus want you to do?

PRAYER – Father, I do not always behave as I should towards my 'neighbours.' Please give me a loving and helpful heart so that my 'neighbour' will see the light of Jesus in my behaviour.

AUGUST 18th

Isaiah 40v28   1 Corinthians 2v9-10   Hebrews 11v9-10

How different is the view from the window on a dull, damp day, or when the wind is blowing and the rain is beating down. So different from a sunny day, but nature needs the wind and the rain, and will benefit from the storm.

Do you tend to feel 'down' when everything seems to go wrong? Think ahead to the future and remember that in God's Word we are told of the glory that awaits us when we come into His presence. What does it matter if you feel 'down?' Look up and forget about the problems that surround your possessions and pleasures here, for far greater joy and pleasure awaits you there. Turn your eyes upon Jesus and you will find a glorious relief from trouble when the sun shines.

PRAYER – Father, how easy it is to let things get me down. Please give me the courage to look up. Thank you that You have promised to lift me up from my concerns.

AUGUST 19th

Zephaniah 3v17   Luke 1v49   Galatians 6v9

When a football team that normally wins, begins to loose goals, the players tend to be discouraged. The first lost goal may cause them to make a supreme effort. Then another goal is lost, then how easy it is to give up making that supreme effort.

When you become despondent, think of all the wonderful things God has done for you in the past. Do you do that ? You seem to be constantly up against opposition but at the same time you have the support of Christian friends and faithful prayers. However, there may be some vital problems that haunt you day and night and although you pray, nothing seems to bring a solution. Seek help and encouragement from supporters and above all, from the Word of God. Have patience and receive the comfort that God is waiting to give you.

PRAYER – Father, I need Your help and the encouragement of others. Please help me to have patience and wait for Your comforting peace and love to strengthen me.

AUGUST 20th

Psalm 91v7   2Corinthians 12v9   Hebrews 6v17-19a

Many pieces of equipment these days are covered by a guarantee. If a part of it goes wrong, we expect the firm to keep the promise made, and replace the damaged part.

Do you doubt God's promises? He always keeps His promises and if He says He will do a thing, He will. Then you have no reason to be concerned. Over and over again, you will read in the Scriptures that the Lord will provide and protect. Over and over again you will read how He will give peace and comfort, joy and love. Why do you not accept these things as your 'guarantee?' It is so necessary for you to 'open up' and be desirous of His Spirit in your life.

PRAYER – Father, why do I resist the truths that You promise in Your Word? Prepare my heart to trust Your promises so that I may experience life in abundance.

AUGUST 21st

Psalm 16v5-6   Psalm 32v8-11   Isaiah 58v11

Swallows have a way of teaching us how to trust. Every winter they migrate to warmer climes, following the same long flight each year. In the spring they return the same way, confident of God's guidance and protection. The older ones usually return to their old nests.

Even when difficulties lie ahead of you, are there times when you hesitate or have doubts that God cares and is in control? God has not forgotten you. It is a good idea to plan the way ahead; work out the timing and get going. Face any problems en route, confident that you know where you are going. Take time to rest occasionally, and so be refreshed in the Lord. He will feed you on His Word and prepare you for the next step of the journey. Keep going; don't give up.

PRAYER – Father, thank you that Jesus will be able to keep me going on my journey. Then You will receive me victoriously into Your presence.

AUGUST 22nd

Romans 14v7-8   1Corinthians 6v19-20   Philippians 1v20-21

It is good that we are able to borrow books from the library. Every subject is covered in most libraries. We must remember however, to look after the books because they do not belong to us, and we want to return them in good condition.

How important it is to remember that your body is a 'temple of the Holy Spirit.' It does not really belong to you, only lent; it belongs to God. Will you remember to take care of it and respect it as 'on loan?' You are human and have a responsibility to keep yourself pure, healthy and rested, living in a healthy Christian way. Also you need to be attractive, presentable, neat and happy, so that people can see a difference in you. Jesus suffered on behalf of us all and now we have a responsibility to return ourselves to the Lord, in 'good condition.'

PRAYER – Father, thank you for my body. Teach me to respect it and use it for Your glory and for the help of others in due course.

AUGUST 23rd

Psalm 23v1-6   Romans 8v37-39   Philippians 4v6-7

In certain parts of Africa today, Christians are multiplying in greater numbers than ever, with enthusiastic determination to share the Gospel. They praise God for this growing development and for the early missionaries who first encouraged them.

Do you stop to think how much you really have to praise God for? He constantly watches over you and whatever trouble you experience, you can look to Him and feel His love, strength, comfort and encouragement. No circumstance can really separate you from this love. It is only you who can cause the separation by creating a situation of anxiety and doubt. Remember those who have taught and guided you into the Christian faith and believe that God will direct you in the path ahead; therein is love.

PRAYER – Father, when I really dedicate myself to You, I know that Your loving hand will direct me and encourage me to witness, even when situations do not seem to be right.

AUGUST 24th

Psalm 34v3-7   Acts 16v25-26   1Peter 4v12-13

Have you ever been to the Royal Tournament and watched the act when horse and rider charge through a burning circle? We sit up in our seats, then watch as they never hesitate but ride through the flames with huge enthusiasm and never a doubt.

You do not need to consider for one moment that God is being unmindful when He takes you through a period of trial, temptation or suffering. Through Jesus, God knows what it is to be tempted. He only allows you to experience just as much as is necessary to improve and perfect you. Your task now is to press on, trust Jesus and be assured that despite all circumstances, He will guide you through.

PRAYER – Father, I tend to hesitate when faced with fiery trials. Please help me to pluck up courage and aim straight through the problems as if they were not there.

AUGUST 25th

Psalm 34v8-10   Ephesians 1v3   Hebrews 4v15-16

At the end of the Second World War there was much rejoicing. Whether in pain or going through a difficult and dangerous experience, everyone rejoiced because there was no more war.

Your reactions must be of continual praise to Jesus and joy in the Lord. Whether you are going through trials or whether you have cause to rejoice, you should be continually praising God. He has your life under His control, all planned out and prepared. Accept correction and draw closer to Jesus as He, in love, rescues you from the hand of the enemy. Rejoice and be glad.

PRAYER – Father, as the enemy quietens down under Your command, I want to rejoice in Your wonderful saving grace.

AUGUST 26th

Matthew 6v33-34   Luke 12v22-26   Philippians 4v11-13

Wild birds find all the food they need in the woods and countryside; they are not anxious. But in the winter it is not so easy. They rely on us to help by sharing seeds etc, in our gardens.

You can be absolutely confident that God will provide everything you need, but not always what you think you need. There will be times when things are 'tight' and we need to be careful. God honours your trust and will bless you. When times are hard He will always help and provide all that is necessary. Will you have faith to believe that this is so? Then, honour, worship and praise the Lord. He will never let you down.

PRAYER – Father, when everything is going well I tend to take things for granted. But when times are 'lean' I look to You and trust You to provide all that is necessary. Thank you, Lord, for Your concern.

AUGUST 27th

Psalm 119v105   Isaiah 30v21   John 8v12

During the Second World War most signposts were removed in the country, so travelling was difficult; even maps were difficult to read. You just had to follow the main roads to reach your destination.

God is continually walking before you and you must keep in that path He has mapped out for you. It requires concentration to be constantly watching for any light or symbol that will help. If you move out of the beam of God's light, you will loose your way and stumble. Sometimes there will be barriers in the way or particular signs will be missing, but you will overcome these if you follow in the light of the Lord; the Word of God. Be alert, awake and enthusiastic all along the way and you will reach the goal, rejoicing and praising the Lord.

PRAYER – Father, please show me the way to go. I am lost without Your guiding signs but know that You will help me in my need.

AUGUST 28th

Romans 8v37   James 1v5   1John 5v4

Certain naturalists have set complicated routes for squirrels raiding bird tables. The route consists of a series of obstacles designed to distract the squirrel. But certain squirrels work them out in due course, and advance to victory.

When you are serving the Lord you must have no fear of obstructions. If you persevere you will have victory, providing you persevere in the name of Jesus. But to have victory you will have to search the Word of God. This will help you to prepare for any satanic attacks. Here you will find encouragement and wisdom and you will praise the Lord in the power of the Holy Spirit in your life. Have you had this experience and do you find obstacles that discourage you? If you follow the Lord, you will be able to do seemingly impossible things.

PRAYER – Father, I give You thanks and praise, for You have called me out of darkness into Your glorious light, enabling me to attempt and conquer the impossible.

AUGUST 29th

2Samuel 22v31-33   Isaiah 12v2   Romans 4v20-21

Newspaper adverts promise so many wonderful products that will encourage us and promote our well being. We tend to get carried away and fall for the temptations.

How many wonderful promises God gives to you. Do you doubt any of them? You need to be utterly committed to Him to know that they are real promises, given for your encouragement in the certainty that they will happen. No matter what your experiences are, God is in control. Satan, with all his tempting ideas, will have no hold upon you, because you are protected from all harm and danger. Don't be discouraged; God will not let your foot slip.

PRAYER – Father, I need regular encouragement to keep me aware of Your wonderful care and protection. Thank you that You are always there in every situation when I search for You with all my heart.

AUGUST 30th

Matthew 15v16-19   2 Corinthians 10v4-5   1John 5v18

There are certain little flies in hot countries known as 'jiggers.' They delight to bite and bury little sacs in peoples toes. If not attended to and removed, the sac enlarges and fills with eggs which turn septic and cause pain and trouble.

What a wonderful thought to think of Jesus in your life. So why do we behave as we do sometimes, letting evil thoughts grow and develop? Let your love for Jesus grow deep into your life and deal with the invasion of unclean things immediately, before they can cause damage. Jesus will not force you into anything but He must be your central thought. Keep in tune with Him.

PRAYER – Father, keep me safe and encourage me to deal with sinful intrusions. Please fill me with Your love and make me a blessing to others.

AUGUST 31st

Isaiah 55v6-9   Romans 15v4   1 Thessalonians 5v10-11

It is unusual to see animals in the wild living on their own. They need company and companionship to share together their experiences. They can learn from one another and encourage one another.

If you try to serve God alone, you will probably be miserable. You cannot do what He expects you to do unless you have advice and help. Have you ever tried to struggle on your own without success? It may be helpful to turn to a counsellor or mature advisor to guide you. But above all, turn to the Scriptures. Jesus will advise. There are times when you really must seek help; never walk alone. Enjoy your church fellowship where you can share and learn and seek advice when necessary. Help and encourage one another.

PRAYER – Father, I need Your help and ask You to guide me to the people who can advise and help me to make the right decisions, instead of trying to 'go it alone.'

SEPTEMBER

SEPTEMBER 1st

Luke 9v23   1Timothy 6v11-21   1Peter 3v4

Mother Teresa was well known as a loving, radiant Christian who spent her life sharing her love with the poor people in India. The love in her life was Jesus' love and it radiated from her face like an ever shining light.

How do you show your love for Jesus today? Basically, only Jesus can create such love through His indwelling Spirit. A love that reveals to others gentleness and peace. To obtain this you must always stay very close to Jesus in all you do and say. You may first have to be pruned, tried and tested in order for any imperfections to be removed. Share your love, seek the lost and make their lives complete.

PRAYER – Father, I want to praise You for the love You have revealed to me through Jesus. I want that love to penetrate into the lives of others. What a privilege it is for me to be part of Your plan.

SEPTEMBER 2nd

Psalm 27v14   Isaiah 41v10   James 1v3-4

Insects don't have any concerns about their lives. They are born or hatched and then without any doubts, seem to know just what to do and where to go, finding food, company, rest and work. How wonderful to be one of God's little creatures. No doubts, no fears, just get on with what you have to do.

Do you hesitate and become doubtful about your well being? Why do you do that when the Lord gives you so many promises in His Word? He is always having to remind you with words of encouragement and promises that He will see you through a situation or give you the necessary strength for a particular task. Often these feelings are given to increase your ability to be patient. The Lord can't really use you unless you are patient. Relax in His love.

PRAYER – Father, as you have called me and accepted me into Your family, so You will take care of me as I seek to do what You require of me. Thank you, Lord.

SEPTEMBER 3rd

2 Corinthians 2v11   Ephesians 6v10-18   1Thessalonians 5v22-23

In many parts of the world today there are many gangs of evil people who are constantly attacking people. They are saturated with evil intents and constantly aim to destroy and kill.

Satan will constantly try to attack you as you innocently seek to live a good, upright life. Are you in danger of contact with such trouble? His aim is to kill and destroy any sign of a love to follow Jesus and you must always be aware of this. You must be constantly on the look out for any satanic activity. Watch what you say and do; even what you think. Be sure that you are equipped with all the protection that the Lord can give you.

PRAYER – Father, fill me daily with the power and protection of Your Holy Spirit which is greater than the power of Satan. Then I will know Your loving peace that Satan can never disturb.

SEPTEMBER 4th

Psalm 56v3-4   Luke 12v25-26   John 14v27

When you have a friend or relative who is likely to be involved in a terrible road accident or natural catastrophe that has just been announced in the news bulletin, it is quite a natural reaction for you to be concerned or worried until more details are available.

Time after time God has to remind you there is absolutely no need for you to worry or be concerned as you travel along the Christian way. He is in complete control of your life and has every situation planned according to your needs. In this way you will be prepared for the work He has for you to do. Are you in the habit of worrying about your family? Have complete trust and confidence in Jesus and place the family in His hands every day. Take an interest in their activities but don't let these interests upset your own walk with the Lord.

PRAYER – Father, what a privilege it is to be filled with Your love. Please help me to remember my family in loving concern, without being anxious.

SEPTEMBER 5th

Romans 12v5-8   Ephesians 4v15-16   1Peter 4v10

An orchestra must be in tune. Each instrument must adapt to the music notes that are applicable to its abilities. All the instruments performing together produce beautiful harmony. But they must be united.

It is very necessary that you realise the responsibilities laid upon you as a Christian. You have a unique gift which God has bestowed upon you and He expects you to use it. Are you conscious of your particular gifting? It will not be the same as your friend; you would not understand his anyway! We are all part of the Body of Christ and need to be a united body. It will be essential for you to know how to use your 'instrument' and then it must be blended together with other 'instruments' to create a wonderful 'harmony' united in the love and service of Jesus, flowing out to others.

PRAYER – Father, please make me an instrument of Your love as I lift up my hands in Your name.

SEPTEMBER 6th

John 14v1-3   Romans 13v11-12   2 Peter 3v8-10

During the Second World War so many husbands and sons had to leave their families to join the armed forces. This caused anxiety for all concerned, but daily routine had to be continued. Then, for some, what excitement when news arrived announcing their safe return.

Jesus is coming back one day and then you will meet Him face to face. Does this thought so excite you that all else becomes unimportant from the point of view of anxiety about your provisions and circumstances here on earth? He will take care of you here, if you put complete trust and confidence in Him. Apart from your anticipation and understanding of Jesus' return, remember to continue with your daily routine and the important responsibility to share this news with others. But always be ready and waiting.

PRAYER – Father, I am so excited as I read in Your Word that one day I will actually meet Jesus, either when He returns or when He calls me. Please help me to be ready as I serve You now.

SEPTEMBER 7th

Jeremiah 29v11   Isaiah 55v11-12   Romans 12v12

When we think of an important event, a wedding, a celebration, a country show etc, it could never happen without a great deal of planning and organising to make it successful.

Does it make you feel humble when you think that God has your life all planned and organised? You have a part to play in His plan and now you are just experiencing part of the programme. You have no idea where He is going to lead you or what part you have to play. You think you do, but you must take one step at a time as His purposes are revealed to you, even if they do not seem right to you. Just be obedient and slot into the right place, so that the overall outcome will be perfect and you will rejoice in all the way the Lord leads you.

PRAYER – Father, thank you for fitting me into Your plan and purpose through this life. I want to play my part and know that this will bring glory to You.

SEPTEMBER 8th

Psalm 51v6-7   Matthew 23v25-28   2 Corinthians 4v16-17

An expertly groomed horse will look really beautiful with a shining coat and bright eyes. The animal looks so alert and attractive. But what about the inside? It could be wild and vicious. This will only be revealed as it performs and is given a free will to act as it desires to do.

It is no good just concentrating on your outward appearance. This is important to a degree, but you must be as concerned about your inward appearance too. Your thinking is important. Do you criticise others in your thinking? Do you complain? Do you pity yourself or desire praise for anything you have done? Praise must be directed to the Lord. Your objective is heaven; you have no real goal on earth.

PRAYER – Father, I ask You to prepare my thoughts and reactions so that I am conscious of Your presence within me. Take me as I am and make me what You want me to be.

SEPTEMBER 9th

Proverbs 3v11-12   Hebrews 12v5-6   Revelations 3v19-20

To undertake the need to lose weight, it is necessary to consider a diet. This calls for strict discipline which does not come easily, but to obtain the required weight loss, you must have discipline.

How often does the Lord have to remind you of the complete necessity for discipline in your Christian life? You do not find it easy to accept some of the things, events and circumstances in which He places you. You should rejoice in these things, not resist them. When you are obedient, responsive and patient, then, and only then, can the Lord really bless. You can then show forth the fruit that He is longing to cultivate within you and you will benefit from your obedience to the Lord.

PRAYER – Father, I do not always listen to You as I should, but I want to be fit and able to serve You. I need Your help.

SEPTEMBER 10th

Isaiah 49v5-6   Philippians 3v12-14   Philippians 4v13

It must be quite a privilege to work for royalty. There will be a period of detailed examination of your application before such a position can be permitted, but the resulting honour and pleasure will be very special.

Do you really appreciate what a privilege it is to be chosen to work for Jesus? Do you realise that it involves carrying on the work that He taught to His disciples? This is a very great responsibility. The disciples had to learn from their mistakes. In the same way you must continually learn from the Lord and accept correction and possible punishment if this is necessary. If you feel inadequate, He will strengthen you by the power of His Spirit. Don't give up.

PRAYER – Father, I am so honoured to be in Your service, but I'm so afraid of making mistakes. Please give me confidence in my work and witness for You.

SEPTEMBER 11th

Acts 20v24   Romans 12v1-2   1John 2v15

In a cross country chase on horseback, it is very necessary to concentrate. You must guide your horse, consider the jumps and remember the course. All have to be thought of if you want to finish the course successfully.

If you are going to work for Jesus you must put your heart and soul into the job. This means that all your thoughts must be geared to Jesus and the course ahead of you. You will have little time to consider other ideas apart from essentials. There will be obstacles en route. These must be approached and tackled with guidance from Jesus. Don't be drawn away as you serve the Lord, but set out to complete the course.

PRAYER – Father, I need to ask You to improve my power of concentration as I travel the course You have set before me to follow. I want to bring praise and glory to You as I go.

SEPTEMBER 12th

Psalm 139v1-4   Ephesians 6v10-13   Hebrews 4v13

Without water plants wither and die. This problem cannot be hidden because the leaves begin to droop, flowers fall and the whole plant looks sick.

You cannot hide anything from God. He knows how you are feeling and what thoughts are going through your mind. He knows all about your human frailty and human weaknesses. It is only by the grace and mercy of God that you can become good and obedient; He alone can give you the ability to be so, by sending Jesus. Temptations will come and you will find yourself continually battling against unpleasant thoughts, but Jesus is far greater than Satan and Jesus has the victory. Do you see now, how you can overcome the evil one?

PRAYER – Father, thank you that I can be assured that You know all about me, my needs, my feelings and thoughts. When I am drained of all my enthusiasm, I am so happy to know that Jesus is waiting to come to my rescue.

SEPTEMBER 13th

Exodus 34v29   Psalm 63v1-4   Hebrews 13v5-6

When an animal is shut up in a cage or shed, it will probably complain and no doubt consider that it has been left abandoned.

Sometimes it is difficult to know that God is near. How often do you have a feeling like that? He may seemingly leave you alone from time to time, so that you can appreciate more what it is to feel His precious and wonderful love surrounding you with a blanket of protection. How great it would be to see Him for a moment and to catch His transforming reflection. Remember the time Moses came down from the mountain. God has not abandoned you even if you cannot see Him. He will never leave you to manage on your own.

PRAYER – Father, although I cannot see You, I know You are there. Please give me faith to trust You, even if I feel abandoned from time to time.

SEPTEMBER 14th

2 Corinthians 1v3-5   2 Timothy 3v10-12   Hebrews 12v2-7

A piece of steak has to be severely beaten before it is grilled, so that the end result is a lovely piece of succulent meat fit to eat.

If you do not experience spiritual beatings and a certain time of suffering, your life would lack so much. When you go through rough patches, do you turn to Jesus for help? In the Scriptures He promises to strengthen and help you. Therefore, you should not be anxious when circumstances are difficult to bear or understand. The end result will be good and will enable you to share your faith with praise and thanksgiving.

PRAYER – Father, it is always difficult to understand Your plans for my life, but please help me to stand up to the hard times and rejoice in the coming results.

SEPTEMBER 15th

Luke 9v62   1 Corinthians 15v58   James 1v2-5

In the kitchen it is essential to be positive about what we are doing, what we are cooking and what the recipe says. If not, we end up in organised chaos with an uncertain meal!

It is very essential to be positive in your faith and not to be swayed into doubt and uncertainty. The Lord has a specific plan for your life and as one of His workers, you must be prepared to be faithful and know what you are doing. Are you sensitive to the slightest indication that you have things organised in your life? To produce a good witness and be able to 'feed' enquirers with the right spiritual 'food,' it is necessary to do things right, with Jesus' help.

PRAYER – Father, I want to get things in order in my spiritual life and I need Your guidance to make sure I've got it right.

SEPTEMBER 16th

Psalm 139v23-24   Proverbs 3v11-12   Isaiah 55v8-9

The mother of children is always aware of their presence. She knows how they react to certain situations and how to deal with them.

How often the Bible reminds us that God is constantly aware of us. Do you realise that He even knows what you are thinking and planning? He knows when you are in control and gently but firmly reminds you that He is the One who should be in control. He must correct you before you go too far away from Him. Jesus will not answer, correct or bless until you are completely in tune with His will and purpose.

PRAYER – Father, You understand my weak thoughts that I consider good. Please give me the desire to seek Your will and follow the Jesus way that is so much better.

SEPTEMBER 17th

Psalm 5v11-12   Isaiah 57v15   2 Timothy 3v16-17

When we order a certain piece of equipment we expect it to arrive complete. If something is missing, the equipment will not work properly.

The Lord wants you in all your completeness, willing to be absolutely in tune with Him, otherwise you will not be fully operational in your Christian walk. Are you conscious of anything missing in your life that would prevent God's Spirit fully operating in your life? Providing you are 'in tune' with Him, He can get to work, with nothing to prevent His love and power and strength flowing through you. He is now waiting for you to be submissive to His will.

PRAYER – Father, I regret that I do not always operate as I should, because I tend to leave something out of my trust in You. Forgive me, Lord, and give me a fresh longing to be complete in You.

SEPTEMBER 18th

Isaiah 49v15-16   Luke 12v6-7   Romans 11v33-36

A child can sometimes get very upset because 'Mummy' is so busy with other urgent demands. The child thinks he or she is forgotten.

Do you sometimes think that God has forgotten you? He may have so many other concerns, but He will never forget you. He is constantly thinking and planning for you. It is quite impossible to imagine what God's mind is like, because our human thoughts cannot possibly consider the greatness of God. Enough for you to know that He has every situation and circumstance under His control. So why do you get anxious and frustrated and try to work things out on your own? Just trust in the God you adore.

PRAYER – Father, I do sometimes think You are not around, so please forgive me and remind me through Your Word, that You will never leave me.

SEPTEMBER 19th

Psalm 121v7-8   Proverbs 15v33   1Corinthians 2v9

Watching the nature films on TV, one marvels at the amazing wild life pictures that are revealed through hidden cameras. The animals and birds have no idea they are being filmed.

Have you ever thought that God is constantly watching you and that He knows everything about you? He is continually promising through His Word, to protect and provide for you because of His great love and mercy towards you. He watches you, even though you are not aware of it. God has made mountains, He made heaven and earth, but He is still able to keep an eye on all your activities too. Make sure you are alert and true, so that He will never find or see you going astray.

PRAYER – Father, thank you for watching all my activities even though I'm not aware of it. Help me to be careful as I seek to be true and faithful.

SEPTEMBER 20th

Psalm 17v6-8   Proverbs 3v11-12   Romans 8v28-32

Generally, a father loves his children and will always want the best for them. There are times however, when he will appear angry, even fierce when he corrects his children for some wrong or unwise act. This is because he loves his child.

Consider God as full of love and compassion for His children. But there are times when you do not recognise His love and He needs to correct you. Are you aware of causing Him distress because of your mistakes? Remember, He promises to provide everything you need, not what you necessarily want. He is sad if you do not accept Him or doubt Him. Let the love of Jesus flow through you to others.

PRAYER – Father, I am so happy that You love me and have so much concern for me. I may not enjoy Your corrections, but please help me to draw near to Jesus who will help me to understand why.

SEPTEMBER 21st

2Corinthians 4v16-17   2Corinthians 12v9-10   Philippians 4v6-7

When a ship gets into rough sea with a strong wind blowing, it tends to toss and roll because it is being buffeted. The captain will be in full control to steer the ship along the right course.

When you are being buffeted around, do you feel cast down and anxious? Do not fear because this is all part of life. Your training is not yet complete until you have been through such experiences. You really must be grateful to God that He wants you to experience difficult times in order to strengthen your faith in Him. Sometimes you are so busy crying to Him, that you do not hear His 'still small voice' answering you. You are growing in spiritual maturity and you will be so much more valuable and useful to Him in the end.

PRAYER – Father, I do not like the 'rough sea' through which I am passing but I do realise that there is an end. Keep me trusting You, now and always.

SEPTEMBER 22nd

Deuteronomy 1v21   Isaiah 42v6-7   John 12v27-28

It would be interesting to know how wild animals feel when they have to spend their lives in a zoo. They may feel 'enclosed' and become restless, but at least they are safe and there is a chance that animals in danger of extinction can be saved in this way.

When problems surround you and you feel the tension, are you likely to get discouraged and despondent? Jesus had many experiences and occasions when He could have given in to pressures and tension but He relaxed, knowing that God was in control. You need to relax too, because Jesus understands. Accept the sovereignty of God and be content to know that all is well when you keep within His will.

PRAYER – Father, When I feel 'enclosed' help me to realise that You are with me to console and comfort me in any concern I may have. Thank you for Your loving care.

SEPTEMBER 23rd

Psalm 119v11   Psalm 119v105   Isaiah 40v8

Entering into dark caves with very little light makes us doubt the ability to continue. But, with care, we can go on if we make use of the little light that is available.

Your standing with God depends, not upon the light you have received through the Scriptures, but of the use you make of what light you have received. How do you deal with the knowledge you have received from the Word of God? It is not always possible to understand some of the accounts you read, particularly in the Old Testament, but concentrate on the parts of Scripture that 'hit' you and learn of those. So you will develop a love for the Word of God and want to share it.

PRAYER – Father, I do pray that You will open up Your Word as I read, so that I can understand what You want to say to me.

SEPTEMBER 24th

Lamentations 3v22-26   Isaiah 58v11   Philippians 4v13

A ladybird is such a tiny insect but it is loved by gardeners because of the good work it does, devouring aphids and other little insects that damage the gardener's flowers and plants.

Do you feel small and insignificant in your service for the Lord? Never the less He loves you and pours out His blessings upon you. He knows that you can be so useful in His world, seeking to guide folk into the way of truth and aiming to do all you can to attack the evil ways of man. Trust Him to know that this is all you need to do. Trust in Jesus, love Him in every situation and be grateful that such love shows you holiness that you never knew before.

PRAYER – Father, it is so thrilling to think that despite my insignificance, I am able to help in some way Your work in the world. Help me to be faithful and consistent as I do the things You have planned for me to do.

SEPTEMBER 25th

Isaiah 28v12   Isaiah 30v15   Isaiah 40v28-31

When the day has been full of busy activity, tiredness takes over. It is not good to push further activities and energy into the days programme, but to rest, relax and stop.

Are there times when you are conscious of the need to completely rest in the Lord? It is necessary for you to 'switch off' and consider a time of complete refreshment in the presence of the Lord, uninterrupted by anything. There will always be calls for a host of requests but it is not always wise to just accept them all. To be totally committed and dedicated to the Lord, you need to be fresh and alert and you cannot be either of these if you try to overcrowd your enthusiasm. Rejoice in the Lord and be upheld and strengthened by time spent in His presence.

PRAYER – Father, I long for a greater desire to serve You but realise too, how important it is for me to rest by the wayside from time to time. Help me to be sensible about this.

SEPTEMBER 26th

Deuteronomy 32v4   Romans 8v37   1Corinthians 15v57

A guard dog is trained to search out the victim, then attack. Having grasped the target, it will 'hang on' in obedience to his master.

Complete obedience to God can only be obtained by attacking all incorrect actions and thoughts and 'hanging on' to them, so that they will not cause any more trouble. At the same time, you must grasp the truth by secure attachment to the Rock, Jesus Christ your Lord. Are you conscious of real victory in this area? Conform to what the Lord desires of you, whatever this may involve and whatever circumstances you are in. The power of the Holy Spirit will help you into the whole truth of what total commitment means.

PRAYER – Father, I need Your wisdom to scent out the undesirable things in my life. Then I will find Jesus, my Rock and my Saviour and I will attach myself to Him in full and complete assurance.

SEPTEMBER 27th

Matthew 4v4   Hebrews 5v8-9   1Peter 5v6-7

A laptop computer can be very useful and helpful if used correctly. But there are points to observe and lessons in obedience. It is essential to hit the right 'key' to get the right response. If not, all kinds of things will happen.

How much and how often you will have to observe obedience as you go through life. Not what you think is obedience, but being absolutely submissive to His will. How often have you misunderstood the true meaning of the word 'obedience?' To obtain this situation you must learn to be humble in all your thoughts and actions. Oh for a heart to praise God, a heart from sin set free. A humble, lowly, contrite heart, believing true and clean.

PRAYER – Father, I want to praise You with a contrite heart and I am so grateful for the love You constantly give to me.

SEPTEMBER 28th

Exodus 34v14   Isaiah 26v13   1John 5v21

There are times when certain folks get absorbed in certain things which overpower other sources of interest, even to the daily necessities of life and important events etc. This is idol worship and needs correction.

How easy it is to make the desires of our earthly human hearts, idols. Although you may not realise it, you worship them. On such occasions do you realise that you have your priorities mixed? Seek the Lord's forgiveness if this is the case and realise that nothing less than complete surrender is sufficient to enable you to be a vessel adequate for your Lord. No priority for pleasures or possessions will suffice. How precious are God's promises which cannot be forthcoming until you are fully committed to Him.

PRAYER – Father, I do not consider myself worthy to receive Your precious love. Forgive me for making my own desires more acceptable than Your love.

SEPTEMBER 29th

Psalm 27v14   1Corinthians 1v27   2Corinthians 12v9-10

In the National Parks of Africa there are times when an animal needs to be checked for some physical problem. This cannot be done until it is 'darted' and quietened. Then some treatment can be given.

To be Christ like you must become weak so that God's strength can shine through you. If you try to live your Christian life on your own, you will 'fall by the wayside,' because self involves impurity. Do you ever feel that you have mastery in what you do on your own? Bring all of yourself to Jesus, then pride and self importance will be 'darted' and you will be left as a weak and empty vessel which Jesus can fill with His Spirit and power to make you strong and loving in His sight.

PRAYER – Father, it is necessary for me to become weak so that my life for You will be strong. Please help me to bend to Your Word and Your treatment for my life.

SEPTEMBER 30th

Exodus 33v12-14   Psalm 25v4-5   Proverbs 4v18

Household machinery is excellent and very helpful if and when you know how it works. Instructions are usually included but these are not always easy to understand, and it helps if someone can explain.

How do you cope with spiritual queries unless they are explained to you? God will not let you fail and often He will direct you to people who can explain your query and give you encouragement by so doing. It is not easy to understand all that the Lord tells us through His Word or in answer to our prayers, but there are stimulating highlights along the way. In response to our encouragement we must realise our responsibilities and be ready to help other folk who are also having queries along the way.

PRAYER – Father, I thank you for all you mean to me and for Your continual answers and words of encouragement. Help me to guide others along the right way as I go.

OCTOBER

OCTOBER 1st

Psalm 104v1-4   Isaiah 9v2   1Peter 1v6-7

When a plane lifts off the runway on a cloudy day, it soon climbs above the clouds and travels in bright sunlight. But it has to travel through the clouds first.

Are there times when you seem to be going through clouds? Switch on to Jesus and He will guide you through into the sunshine above. Do not try to negotiate the clouds on your own or you may take the wrong course. It may seem unpleasant at the time but you must keep going and not give up. If you keep below the clouds, there are beautiful views of the countryside which will attract you, but it is so much better to climb higher and share the joy of the sunshine above.

PRAYER – Father, what a thrill it is to rise above the clouds and to know Your encouragement as I rise higher into the light of Your presence.

OCTOBER 2nd

Isaiah 1v18   Isaiah 44v22   1John 1v5-9

When we make a mistake and perhaps accuse someone of something they have not done, we may get cross because we consider they are wrong. But when we discover the truth, we feel guilty.

How wonderful to know that as you come to God for forgiveness, He responds to your pleading. It is not natural to be good and honest and understanding, but you have a new beginning when you come to Jesus. Do you now find that God is able to work out His purposes through you? But still there are faults and it is only by God's mercy that you can now understand your faults, and can be sympathetic with the folks you may have upset.

PRAYER – Father, I plead for Your understanding in my faults and failures. Thank you, that in Your mercy You will forgive.

OCTOBER 3rd

Mark 15v37-39   2 Timothy 4v18   1Peter 2v9-10

From time to time we hear about accidents with cave searchers. Immediately help comes to hand and often explorers have to be dug out of the caves. It would be impossible for them to get out alone. They must have help.

It is natural for us all to sin but when Jesus died, the temple curtain was torn from top to bottom, thus enabling us to have direct access to God, an opportunity to be rescued from the consequences of sin. Are you grateful that you have been given this opportunity? You will now be in the light. Why do so many people prefer to stay in the dark?

PRAYER – Father, as the curtain was torn and the way opened up for me to be rescued, so I come to You with grateful thanks for Your loving care and concern. Use me now, to help serve in a needy world.

OCTOBER 4th

Matthew 5v14-16   Acts 2v1-4   2Corinthians 3v18

A whole lot of empty glasses placed before a group of thirsty people is not very helpful. They need to be filled with water.

Do you realise how necessary it is to consider yourself as just a vessel to be used in the service of the Lord? It is only in this way that God can work through you. An empty vessel does not help His work to go forward, but creates a barrier and prevents the love of God from getting through and shining out to radiate His glory and so bring love and satisfaction to those around you. Have concern and be totally committed to Him. Operate as part of the Body of Christ.

PRAYER – Father, take me, fill me and use me in Your service. Use me to help those who are thirsty for Your help.

OCTOBER 5th

Psalm 8v3-5   Psalm 42v11   1Peter 5v7

Patients resting in the intensive care unit in hospital are watched carefully by the nurse and any change is immediately reported to the doctor. The patient can be certain that he is cared for.

Isn't it a wonderful comfort to know that in every circumstance God is continually watching you so that you can be assured that He will not let you experience anything that will not be in some way for your good. Do you believe that God always cares for you in this way? Have patience and wait as you go through the necessary period of recovery.

PRAYER – Father, I am grateful for Your special care and pray that as I recover, You will be constantly by my side.

OCTOBER 6th

Mark 11v22-24   Luke 1v37   Hebrews 11v6

There are times when a certain house seems just right, but in no way can we afford it. So we make every effort to raise enough capital to achieve our desire, and have faith to believe that it will work out if this is right.

However difficult and impossible circumstances appear to be, you can be assured that if you really do have enough faith, God will bring anything to pass if He wishes to. Are you strengthened by this fact or do you have doubts? Be constantly alert and 'work out your salvation.' Listen to God, be obedient to His Word and follow Jesus wherever He leads you, confident and faithful as you call out to Him; your hope is in Him alone.

PRAYER – Father, please guide me in my decisions and in my daily deliberations. Give me wisdom as I trust in You, my Rock in times of decision.

OCTOBER 7th

Psalm 25v8-9   Proverbs 16v9   James 1v5

Employed in a certain occupation, you are unable to be very helpful until someone has trained you to do the particular task you have been employed to do. You have to concentrate, be enthusiastic and be patient. Then you will understand and be able to work well.

It is no good thinking that you can guide or teach yourself how to live the Christian life. You must be directed by God through church fellowship or contact and advice from wise counsellors or prayer partners. God knows where He wants you to be, and what He wants you to do. Concentrate or you may lose the way. He knows all the answers to your queries, so keep in touch, study the guide lines in Scripture and work with enthusiasm.

PRAYER – Father, to You be all glory and wisdom and power. Thank you for the help I have received. May my ministry and witness for You be fruitful and encouraging wherever You place me.

OCTOBER 8th

Isaiah 35v3-4a   Daniel 10v19   Acts 20v24

When confronted with a new experience, we tend to doubt our ability and avoid involvement, or if we decide to tackle it, we may be fearful.

There is no place for fear or doubt in your walk with Jesus. He is always there to protect you, even if you are entering new experiences in your Christian life. Your basic human reaction causes you to hesitate but it is necessary for you to follow wherever the Lord leads. Have you got a new experience that causes you concern? Try praising the Lord for His wisdom in making you understand. Jesus surrounds you with love, peace and joy and these things will surpass any doubts you may have. Fit into His tapestry of design, even if it is a new experience, and praise Him for His loving kindness and strength.

PRAYER – Father, when I encounter new experiences, please help me to be patient and learn from You, so that I will not be fearful, but will seek to understand what You are trying to teach me.

OCTOBER 9th

Ephesians 1v11-12   Ephesians 4v11-12   1Peter 4v12-13

In the autumn it is usual to see fallen leaves tossing and whirling about everywhere. This is particularly noticeable in the woods, but eventually they will settle down and rot making a good nutritious base for new growth of plants and trees the following year.

Do you sometimes feel that God is 'tossing' you about? Be encouraged that in the 'tossing' you are being prepared for a particular source of supply in service for the Lord. You need to fit into God's plan and purpose for you, helping to create wholesome spiritual input for future generations. So never begrudge the 'tossing' but keep constantly in touch with Jesus, to be guided into your specific ministry in the days to come.

PRAYER – Father, I want to accept Your plans for my life, because you have a particular task for me to do. So I thank you for any 'tossing' You need to do in preparation.

OCTOBER 10th

Galatians 3v26-28   Ephesians 4v4-6   1John 3v1-2

What fun it is when a family meets together for special family occasions. Often it is the first time for some years since this happened and there is cause to celebrate.

How wonderful to know that in Christ we are all one big family and the same love is poured out upon us all. God is your Father; do you enjoy special times in His presence? You can talk to Him knowing that he will listen and will react accordingly. Week by week you will meet with your spiritual brothers and sisters to praise your Heavenly Father and this will be a time of celebration as you gather in your special fellowship. Praise the Lord for our unity in Spirit one with another.

PRAYER – Father, thank you for Your family and for including me as one of Your children. I am so grateful for the privilege.

OCTOBER 11th

Acts 17v11   Colossians 1v16-17   2Timothy 3v16-17

There are so many new gadgets on the market these days, but if we are given one without instructions, we have no idea how to use it or even what it is for.

You are unlikely to discover what life is all about by asking yourself, because you did not create yourself. So how can you know what you were made for. Is this a puzzle to you? The only answer is to read the 'manual.' Turn to the Scriptures and you will find all you need to know, how you were made and what you were made for. God, your Creator, explains it all and Jesus is 'on hand' to help you. Try it.

PRAYER – Father, I get confused when I try to sort myself out, but You know me and I pray You will give me the wisdom to sort out my life and use it as You have planned.

OCTOBER 12th

Job 22v21   Psalm 119v165   Isaiah 26v12

Inanimate trees never get anxious about the future. If they did, there would be a lot of anxious trees in the world, wondering if they were to be cut down eventually and whether they would be used to make furniture.

Jesus wants you to have peace concerning the future. It is so easy to question God if plans seem difficult for you to understand. Do you sometimes wonder what your future holds? God knows what He is doing and your place is to conform with His will and be what He wants you to be and do. Then you will slip into that plan without a struggle. God will organise any necessary preparation and you will feed on His Word and keep in touch through daily prayer and communication.

PRAYER – Father, thank you that I do not need to be anxious about my future because You know how I will be used. Help me to feed on Your Word and thank you that Jesus is always ready to help me.

OCTOBER 13th

Psalm 138v6   Isaiah 57v15   1Peter 5v5-6

It is easy to fall in the street on an uneven pavement and this can be very embarrassing if people are passing by. One just has to 'bottle pride' and respond to any helping hand available.

We are constantly being reminded of the word 'humble.' How necessary it is for you to be humble in your Christian walk, so that the Lord can work out His purposes through you. Do you realise that He wants to use you to guide others to faith in Jesus? How often do you humble yourself when people respond to your gentle persuasion? You want folks to praise Him, not you. You are just a vessel and if you keep getting in the way, you become a hindrance rather than a help.

PRAYER – Father, please stop me blocking the way of Your loving concern for folk. I want to help but it is necessary and right that I give You all the glory.

OCTOBER 14th

Deuteronomy 8v3   Hebrews 2v12   Hebrews 13v6-8

These days everyone seems to need entertainment of one kind or another so that worldly activities seem to take priority over everything, and many urgent and important occasions often get neglected.

Your concern should no longer be involved with worldly activities to the extent of allowing them to take priority over Jesus. You have to live and work in the world; this is your mission field. Do you display Jesus in your character so that your presence in the world has real meaning? Jesus will never fail to penetrate through your life if you let Him. Mean what you say and do what you mean in the name of Jesus.

PRAYER – Father, please help me to be a keen and enthusiastic missionary as I seek to show the love of Jesus amongst those who consider worldly entertainment and amusements more important than God in their lives.

OCTOBER 15th

Psalm 90v2   Isaiah 60v19-20   Jeremiah 31v3

Watching a beginner in the swimming pool, it is interesting to see how the instructor always has his or her arms available to support and rescue where necessary.

How comforting it is to know that God's everlasting arms are constantly beneath you and to know that His strength is abundant and sufficient for you in every situation. Have there been special times when you have felt the comfort of God's arms protecting you during a certain situation? There may be times when darkness seems to surround you and you feel deserted and alone. Then you can be sure that God will surround you if you will trust Him. Consider the needs of others and hold your arms out, radiating God's love to them too.

PRAYER – Father, I need the comfort and protection of Your everlasting love. Help me to pass that love on so that others may experience Your arms of loving care as well.

OCTOBER 16th

Colossians 1v29   2Timothy 3v16-17   Jude v20-21

Young seedlings when they begin to grow, concentrate on the job of developing. They depend on the goodness of the soil and water then complete their growth, each plant according to its particular variety.

You always need to remember that your work for the Lord needs to be sincere, honest and enthusiastic. Do you concentrate on the task God has set aside for you to do? Depend on good 'soil' found in the Scriptures. Absorb and develop the nourishment you obtain there, to help your Christian life to materialise to full maturity. Then you will develop the special gift of ministry and witness for which you have been made. Do not be distracted by adverse conditions; just keep near to the Lord.

PRAYER – Father, I want to grow strong in Your love and follow the instructions from Your Word. Let me develop and mature so that I can bring pleasure to those who put their trust in You.

OCTOBER 17th

Psalm 32v11   Philippians 4v4   1John 5v4

At the victory day celebrations following the Second World War, there was great rejoicing in the country and people everywhere joined in the various celebration activities. There were street parties and parades and everyone was happy with everyone else.

You do not need to wait for any special occasions, but continually rejoice in the Lord. Do you do that? It is not always easy to feel a sense of joy when things seem to go wrong for no particular reason. Are you spending a regular time with Jesus or do you need to spend more time celebrating over the victory He brought to us all when He died at Calvary? Think about this, then you will want to join in the victory celebrations too.

PRAYER – Father, I want to celebrate victory in Jesus. Now I am free from the terrors of the evil one because Jesus has overcome and I share His joy. Thank you that He was obedient to Your desires.

OCTOBER 18th

1 Chronicles 29v11   Hebrews 10v22   1John 1v8-9

When foot and mouth epidemics occur, it is necessary for farmers to have large containers at the gate of the farm for visitors to thoroughly immerse their feet in disinfectant before entering. This will destroy any possibility of further infection.

Are you able to draw near to God in all sincerity? You must be totally immersed in God's love in order to destroy any devastating thoughts and ideas. Then you will be able to receive the peace and love that He is waiting to give you. There is so much sin and destruction in the world and you need to be totally cleansed before entering into the presence of the Lord. Be free of all things that would limit His power in your life.

PRAYER – Father, when I take the right precautions I will be free to enter into Your presence. Show me the way I need to go amidst the chaos of our world so that I may be able to help in some way to serve in Your world.

OCTOBER 19th

Psalm 73v24-26   Colossians 4v2   2Timothy 3v16-17

There are certain items that are important in our diet in the form of vitamins etc. These are present in certain foods but it is sometimes advisable to take extra in tablet form.

What are your basic thoughts about God? He is the source of strength and power that you need daily. He will protect you from all fear and alarm. No doubt you spend a daily time with Him and this is good, but it is probably necessary for you to take some extra time in prayer and Bible study, to provide an increase in your basic needs. As you do so, you will grow and develop in your faith, and your walk with the Lord will be so much more meaningful and fruitful.

PRAYER – Father, thank you that I can build up my faith in You, as I spend more time in Your presence and in Your Word. Use me as I grow stronger to be an encouragement to others too.

OCTOBER 20th

Jeremiah 15v16   Psalm 119v105   Colossians 3v16

Many years ago there were no books to read and study. Even today many people in the world cannot read even if they have books. Without this opportunity learning is not easy. Then even with books, there is the language problem.

How much do you depend on the Word of God? This should be your 'text book' day by day. How can you follow Jesus without daily instructions? He tells you where to go, what to do and how to do it. The Word of God will shape your character and your attitude to others. It is full of instructions and guide lines. You need to understand what the Bible has to say to you, then put into action all that you hear. Let it penetrate into you, regardless of any complications that may surface.

PRAYER – Father, thank you for Your precious Word. Help me to understand all that You need me to know and then to act upon it.

OCTOBER 21st

Romans 8v17a   Ephesians 3v14-18   1John 3v1

Families usually stick together. These days they are much more wide spread than they used to be when they all tended to live in the same village or town and were born, married and buried there.

Do you ever stop to realise that you are a child of God? As your Father, He will always be concerned about you and will want the best for you. In so doing, He may often correct you and expect obedience. Be a 'credit' to your Heavenly Father and show respect for others in a way that would not have been possible without His loving care and training.

PRAYER – Father, what an honour to call You Father. Thank you that as Your child I have that special privilege of being part of Your family. Thank you for Your loving care.

OCTOBER 22nd

Psalm 46v10   Isaiah 26v3-4   Philippians 4v7

Away from the busy towns and the hustle and bustle of daily life, escape to the rolling mountains of Scotland or Wales. Up there in the solitude, there is peace that will relax the mind and the soul. Perfect peace.

There should be perfect peace when you rest completely in the Lord. Do you have that overwhelming peace in the Lord? When you are in the centre of His will there is peace, even if it is surrounded by disturbances of one kind or another. These things cannot harm you because God has promised to keep and protect you and He always keeps His word. So whatever is going on around you, be still, experience the peace of the Lord; a peace that passes all understanding.

PRAYER – Father, I long for that peace that only You can give. Help me to be still and know that You are God, spreading Your love over all who put their trust in You. Thank you Lord.

OCTOBER 23rd

Psalm 37v16   Proverbs 30v8-9   Hebrews 13v5-6

These days everyone concentrates on finances, to cover living expenses. A longing for everything they want but do not necessarily need. Birds and animals do not worry about these things.

Do you find it natural to centralise everything round the need for finance? Without enough money you wonder how you are going to manage. You will need money because this is a necessity, but when will you realise that God knows you have to have enough money to keep going honestly. You need to spend wisely, then God will honour you and send what you need when you need it. Just praise Him that His 'bank' never runs dry.

PRAYER – Father, thank you that You know my needs and will provide what is necessary at the right time. I pray for so many that do not have all they need. Help me to show concern.

OCTOBER 24th

2Timothy 3v8-9   Hebrews 12v1-3   1Peter 5v8-11

When within a group, decisions have to be made about certain things, there are bound to be those who disagree. Opposition can cause a lot of trouble and complications.

Are you conscious that there are those who are in opposition to what you are doing in your walk with the Lord? This may be the case, but it is so essential for you to take your instructions from the Lord. To say you will be obedient is one thing, but to mean it is another thing. At this point Satan will take every opportunity to unbalance you. If you stay close to Jesus and spend time in God's Word, there will be no impact from satanic sources. You are surrounded by the love of Jesus, through His Spirit. Those who oppose you cannot destroy this truth.

PRAYER – Father, I am so confronted by opposition and I get confused. Please give me the desire to draw closer to Jesus and feel His perfect protection and love as I seek to follow Your way for my life.

OCTOBER 25th

John 14v21   Ephesians 3v17-21   1John 2v3-6

Watch a flock of sheep with young lambs scampering hither and thither. Each mother knows her own baby and will discard another. There is great love demonstrated here.

Is your love for Jesus such that you think about Him every day as you seek His presence? Jesus is always with you with a great concern for you to follow Him and witness in the place of God's appointment for you. When you really do love Him, He will reveal His love to you, a love upon which you can depend to uphold you in your ministry. This love is so powerful that it will give you inner strength, peace and joy that will keep you from falling.

PRAYER – Father, I want to obey Jesus because I love Him and when I obey, I know this will bring glory to You, my Father God.

OCTOBER 26th

Isaiah 40v28-31   2Corinthians 6v16   Ephesians 1v4-6

When something is made, there must be a creator. He has probably designed his creation with great care. Then he is delighted to see it being used and enjoyed. If it is not used correctly however, the creator will be greatly disappointed.

It is so wonderful to know that God is our Creator. Do you realise that He has made you for a special purpose? Your body is in fact, a vessel and you have a responsibility to look after it. Keep away from evil ways and use it as designed to be used. God, your Creator, should be respected at all times. Be faithful and obedient in your ministry and you will be greatly rewarded in the days ahead.

PRAYER – Father, I am so encouraged to know that You created me. Help me to be faithful in my behaviour and fit for use in the task You have intended for me to do.

OCTOBER 27th

Psalm 144v15   Proverbs 8v34-35   Proverbs 16v20

A walk through woodland reveals a picture of happiness. Birds singing, a gentle breeze in the trees and a meandering stream trickling gentle through this scene of utter beauty. You have to feel happy.

Happiness in your Christian life is not possible without complete obedience to the Lord and a longing to be like Jesus. How often do you find a sense of happiness in nature? Ofcourse there will be some rough patches and difficulties and there may be sickness and disappointments. Nature here on earth is never perfect. But you can overcome so much by having faith in the beauties of life that will bring happiness. Never give up.

PRAYER – Father, although there are so many sad things in life, there can be happiness too. I want to dedicate my life to You and experience that special happiness that only You can give.

OCTOBER 28th

Psalm 43v5   Isaiah 49v14-16   2Corinthians 4v7-9

Elderly people living alone, often feel lonely and forgotten. They need fellowship and occupation that will keep their minds active and alert.

On occasions when your spirit feels low and things seem to be at a standstill or irritate you for some reason, do you feel that God has deserted you? Maybe He has for a while, but this is just to teach you a lesson, or correct you for some reason. But He will never forget you, even when you feel this way. Trust Him. No matter how crushed and unwanted you feel, don't despair. God is aware of the fact and will step in at just the right time.

PRAYER – Father, when I feel lonely and despondent, please lift me up. Encourage me and give me the desire to encourage other lonely people too.

OCTOBER 29th

Luke 16v10   Hebrews 11v6-10   James 1v12

Someone may take endless hours preparing a project like a painting or a flower arrangement, to perfection. When questioned why, the artist or arranger will assure you that it may not be in the limelight, but all the same, he wants it to be perfect.

Have you ever realised how important it is for you to perfect your work for the Lord, even if it is not for prominent display? Before you are permitted by God to do a greater presentation, He will test you with a less prominent one first. As your faith is tested, you will have a greater willingness to trust the Lord. Try to consider this truth.

PRAYER – Father, please show me how to do the task You set before me with greater faith. I am willing for You to 'test me out' and I will follow where You lead.

OCTOBER 30th

Psalm 37v7   2Peter 3v8-9   James 5v7-8

Watching herds of buffalo on the African plains at the time of the migration, one notices a stirring amongst the animals. The time has come to move on and they are restless to be on the move.

It is human nature to become impatient and restless from time to time. Do you have that feeling of restlessness when you are waiting for God to answer your prayer and do you get impatient? You need to remember that with God time is immaterial and you must learn to be more patient as you wait for His will and purpose for your life to unfold. In due course He will make it clear, but will not act until He is certain that you are ready.

PRAYER – Father, I am sorry that I get impatient and restless. As I wait for You to prepare me for the way ahead, give me the ability to wait, confident that everything is under control.

OCTOBER 31st

Psalm 31v3   James 1v22   1John 5v1-4

When a game is played over a period of time, it tends to become boring and uninteresting. The only way to avoid this situation is to have a change.

How often do you find yourself attending church services out of habit rather than desire? You will hear God speaking to you through His Word, but now you need to respond and get into action. There will now be no time to become bored. Go forward and respond to what God is calling you to do and seek the presence of Jesus to guide you along the way. Help others to see that life is exciting, not boring, unless you allow it to be so.

PRAYER – Father, I will never be bored when You are directing me and when Jesus is my Guide. Help me to find the interests in life that You are wanting me to know about.

NOVEMBER

NOVEMBER 1st

Joshua 24v24   Proverbs 3v5-6   John 10v14-16

When we meet friends in the street we want to stop and chat with them. We want to hear what they have to tell us and we want to share our latest news too.

When you are in the presence of Jesus, do you wait anxiously to hear what He has to say and do you enjoy telling Him about your activities? When He tells you what to do, you need to obey and consider His way, not yours. He promises to protect, direct and provide, so do not doubt Him. If you follow this principle, things will fit into place and you will go from day to day accepting whatever experience He wants you to have, rejoicing in the privilege of following Jesus.

PRAYER – Father, I am not always obedient and I am sorry; please forgive me. Thank you that Jesus is always ready to show me the way. Please help me to listen to Him.

NOVEMBER 2nd

Isaiah 12v2-3   1Peter 2v21   Jude 24-25

There are times when we can spend hours preparing a special meal for a special occasion. Then at the last minute disaster strikes. Either something burns or the vegetables do not turn out as you had planned. What a calamity!

Human nature tries to take over and destroy the training that God has planned for you. Do you sometimes get upset or impatient when this happens? You must concentrate more upon Jesus. He suffered so much and had so many disasters in His life as He sought to make life so special for us all. He was so patient and this is your example to follow. Patience and peace, regardless of temptations and sin surrounding you. Let the love of Jesus take over as you draw near to Him day by day.

PRAYER – Father, when my feeble efforts get upset and spoilt, may I keep calm and realise that through the love of Jesus, all will be well in the end and I must not panic.

NOVEMBER 3rd

1Samuel 3v8-10   Proverbs 19v20-21   Mark 9v7

A pet animal, a dog, cat or horse, for example, will always be on the alert and listening for their master to call them. Generally, they will respond but there may be occasions when they are obstinate.

It is essential to be always listening for God to speak. Are you listening for God to call you? How can you know what He wants you to do if you do not concentrate on what He is trying to say? How loving and patient He is with us all as He corrects and brings to our notice, things that we need to put right. Now He can train you and prepare you for a wonderful future.

PRAYER – Father, please forgive me for the times I do not obey you, even if I hear You speaking to me. Help me to be more ready to listen.

NOVEMBER 4th

John 14v1-4   2Timothy 1v8-10   1Peter 4v12-13

When it is necessary to have a stay in hospital, it is always good when you are told that you are now fit enough to go home.

Are you excited to know that you suffer with Christ in so many ways? You have experienced some discouragement although nothing compared with what Jesus experienced. His suffering enabled you to be free and now you are 'ready to go home' and you should be excited about this and anxious to know what God has in store for you. Concentrate on developing a more lovable character which will really reveal Jesus in your life, and reflect His glory. Walk in the Spirit with joy in your heart.

PRAYER – Father, I am conscious that Jesus suffered so much for me. Now He is with You and one day will reveal His glory as He returns to planet earth. What a wonderful day that will be.

NOVEMBER 5th

Isaiah 40v28-31   1Corinthians 12v4-7   Galatians 5v22-25

Watching a herd of wildebeest crossing a river, often seen on television nature programmes, one sees from time to time a doubting wildebeest as he hesitates. This is so often fatal as he gets thrown and trampled on by the oncoming herd.

Have you ever been bowled over by enormous tasks or problems which have caused you to hesitate? Be thankful that the Lord understands and is ready to give the necessary strength for you to cope. Never have doubts about the way you are going but pray that the fruits of the Spirit may be revealed in your work and witness for Jesus. Use every moment to reveal His love through your life while you still have the opportunity. Don't let the crowd trample on you.

PRAYER – Father, I want to go the way You lead and I pray that You will keep me from hesitating and doubting when obstacles crop up. May I keep going in faith, believing that You will give me the necessary will power.

NOVEMBER 6th

Psalm 32v8   John 14v15-17   2Timothy 3v16-17

It is necessary for some of us to take special medication for certain reasons. These basically do the trick, but generally need repeating every day or week to acquire the necessary effect.

Are you conscious of the wonderful power of the Holy Spirit in your life? Do you realise that you need a daily 'top up' to keep you alive in the Spirit? Be guided day by day as you search the Scriptures and spend time in the presence of the Lord. He will enable you to walk along the way of His choice but will give you the ability, through His Spirit, to follow correctly. God will watch you and correct you. Be sensitive and responsive.

PRAYER – Father, without Your Spirit in my life, I cannot possibly manage. Thank you for Your care and concern. I realise how much I depend upon the Spirit and also that I need to receive a daily portion.

NOVEMBER 7th

Romans 8v23-25   Colossians 1v9-14   James 1v4

Bird watchers spend a lot of time in 'hides' or under trees, as they wait quietly for the birds to fly naturally, ignoring the presence of people. The bird watchers have to be very patient.

Patience makes a difference to your character. When you have learnt this lesson, God will be able to use you to a greater extent by letting His praise flow through you. How often do you stop to consider whether you are being patient enough? You will have to come right down to ground level, as it were, and you will really have to depend more on Jesus every day. This is a great privilege and you will want to praise Him for His wonderful care and love.

PRAYER – Father, how thrilling it is to just wait patiently to see what You are going to show me. I praise You for all the exciting experiences that lay ahead of me.

NOVEMBER 8th

Isaiah 41v13-14   Ephesians 6v10-17   1John 5v3-4

If we try to attempt to do something that we have never tried before, what a comfort it is if someone who is familiar with the task is standing by our side to guide us.

What a complete comfort it is to know that the Lord is standing right beside you. Are you aware of the fact that He is aware of everything that happens to you? He is also aware of your reaction to life in all its circumstances. He will be aware of how much faith you have when the going is rough. He is there and you just have to hold out your hand and touch Him. Power, confidence, strength and peace will then flow through you. Go forward and know that in the name of Jesus, you will now have the victory over any satanic plans.

PRAYER – Father, I am so relieved to know that You are right by my side. Now I have confidence to tackle the task that I did not understand, knowing that You will show me the way.

NOVEMBER 9th

Psalm 103v2-5   Romans 10v11-13   2Timothy 3v16-17

Having to go to the doctor with a complaint you don't understand, you have to believe his diagnosis and agree to take medicine you know nothing about, to cure your ailment. This is faith.

When you have a spiritual problem what do you do? There is only one answer; turn to God. He is the One between your faith and your circumstances. If you have problems in this area, seek help from those who can help and advise. You will find help in the Scriptures that will encourage your faith. You may not understand all that you read but when God orders a 'prescription,' it will only be suitable for your particular needs. So accept His treatment and anticipate a cure.

PRAYER – Father, how grateful I am to You that I can find a cure. I do not always understand Your treatment but I do realise that You know what You are doing.

NOVEMBER 10th

Deuteronomy 7v6   John 15v16   Hebrews 11v6

When we shop for vegetables or fruit, we tend to turn over the display stock to chose the items most suitable for our needs. We trust that they are wholesome and good so that we can enjoy them.

God chose you, and you must make an effort to please Him. Do you try to please God by your own efforts? This is really quite impossible. It is the Holy Spirit within you that will give you the ability to please God and you must not block the way. You belong to God now, and if He wants to test you, 'let go and let God.' Respond to His call and be grateful.

PRAYER – Father, I am so privileged to be chosen by You in Your service. I want to bring You pleasure as I seek to fulfil Your will with the gifts You have bestowed upon me.

NOVEMBER 11th

Exodus 23v20   Isaiah 40v3   Luke 1v76-77

Before any great or small event it is always necessary to have preparation. If not, so many details will be missed out, and this will effect the main event.

Are you prepared for the wonderful task of serving the Lord? He still has some preparation work to do on you before He considers you worthy and fit for the task He has for you to do. Although you might feel that you are being 'put through the mill' sometimes, you can be encouraged by the wonderful promises in God's Word, to follow Jesus. He will provide the necessary strength and light to guide you. What more could you wish for?

PRAYER – Father, I realise that I cannot set out alone on my pilgrim way without preparation and Your guiding hand through Jesus and Your precious Holy Spirit. Help me to be faithful.

NOVEMBER 12th

Romans 7v18-19   James 1v12-14   1Peter 5v8

Temptations surround us in every direction these days and so often we have the urge to leave the 'straight and narrow' and follow the temptation. This will lead us into all kinds of difficulties.

How often have you listened to temptations and been encouraged to act, but at the same time you have wanted to follow the Lord? If you have chosen to follow the Lord and to keep on the direct path, you will gradually grow into the character of Christ. Growth will be slow, but don't give up. It is quoted that if you have never been tempted to be bad, then you cannot claim to be good! Satan will go for your weakest points, so make sure you sort them out as you go.

PRAYER – Father, please give me the courage to make the right decisions and choices as I seek to follow You, and reveal Christ's character in all I do and say.

NOVEMBER 13th

John 15v12-13   Ephesians 5v1-2   1John 3v11

It is sad when we observe families that always seem to be 'at war' with one another. They seem to have lost the art of loving and can only find fault.

Do you find it difficult to love your family? Jesus had so much love that He gave His life for you and me. In His devotion to His Father, He suffered so much. If you are going to love like Him, you have sometimes got to be prepared to accept suffering and undesirable situations if you are really prepared to love other people in the way He loved you. You will need to be patient and steadfast, with a deep longing to be really useful in your love for others. Rest in the Lord and seek to understand one another.

PRAYER – Father, please give me that urgent desire to love like Jesus loved and to have more concern for those who do not love.

NOVEMBER 14th

2Samuel 22v31-34   2Corinthians 1v20-22   Titus 1v1-2

There are occasions when promises are very special and need to be faithfully observed. When a promise is made and then forgotten, it can cause much pain and disappointment. The person concerned cannot be relied upon.

How encouraged are you when you read about God's promises in Scripture? It is as if the Lord is preparing you for a difficult experience through which He wants you to pass. He is giving you words of promise and encouragement to cope with the situation. Now you can face any danger or difficulty, because Jesus is right beside you, even 'holding your hands.' A hand speaks as it touches. Do not hesitate or doubt, for Jesus has promised to be with you. He keeps His promise; you keep yours.

PRAYER – Father, please help me to be confident in the promises I find in Your Word and help me to keep the promises I make to You.

NOVEMBER 15th

Psalm 73v28   Isaiah 40v26   John 8v12

Flying gives one a sense of awe. In a clear blue sky you look down on the country below and notice so much detail, which becomes less distinct as the plane rises higher. Above a cloud covering, nothing to see but blue sky and sunshine. The world has disappeared.

How do you see the world around you? Do you notice the details or are they too indistinct for you to decipher? As you put your trust in Jesus, He will lift you up into a spiritual atmosphere which will enable you to view the world from a distance. As you draw nearer to God, the things of the world will become more and more indistinct, but as you rise above the clouds below, into the sunshine of God's love, you will be filled with awe and wonder.

PRAYER – Father, as I rise into Your presence, fill me with Your love that will overcome all the worldly scenes and clouds of doubt I am experiencing.

NOVEMBER 16th

1Timothy 4v7-8   2Timothy 2v3-4   Hebrews 12v11

Army cadets have to be trained and they do not find this easy. Energetic physical exercises and long tiring marches. Strict discipline and obedience. All this for the making of a reliable, strong soldier.

Are you trained and ready to be enrolled in God's army? To be prepared for action in the Christian life, training is necessary, with a good deal of 'pruning' if you are going to fit into the task the Lord has for you to do. You will find that God's Word will become your 'text' book. Here you will find instructions and encouragement; a challenge to guide you in your training. One day Jesus is going to return and you need to be ready for that great occasion, confident that God alone knows the date. Be ready, keep marching and utilise your training to share the love of God wherever you go, looking towards that glorious day.

PRAYER – Father, thank you for Your training programme in my life, and for the love of Jesus that guides me in discipline and obedience.

NOVEMBER 17th

1Corinthians 1v9   Ephesians 3v17-19   1John 1v3-4

There are times when we are alone and long for company; someone to talk to and with whom we can share a problem or a moment of exciting news. There are a lot of lonely people in the world in situations like this.

Do you have moments when you long to have someone with whom you can share some news? Draw near to Jesus, because He is always ready to listen to you and to share what you have to say. As you take this step, you will find yourself more dependent upon Him and then you will cease planning out your own way. You will become less frustrated and more conscious of His guidance in your life, revealing each step, one at a time. Now you will not have time to feel lonely.

PRAYER – Father, I praise You as each step in my life is revealed when I spend time sharing with Jesus. Help me to consider so many other folk, so that I can be used to help them and share the blessings I have.

NOVEMBER 18th

Matthew 6v13   Mark 14v37-38   1Corinthians 10v13

A toy mouse on a piece of string can be dragged in front of a pet cat to create amusement, but what does the cat think? He is being tempted into chasing a mouse which isn't a mouse at all!

Temptation is a constant source of battle and no matter what, you cannot escape it. Do you find it a problem to differentiate between temptation and punishment? When you are tempted, do not try to sort this out on your own. Turn to a trusted counsellor, but above everything else, turn to the Lord. He will uphold you, and your faith will be stronger for the experience.

PRAYER – Father, please don't let me fall under temptation. I give You praise and thanksgiving because I know that You will help me to overcome.

NOVEMBER 19th

Matthew 12v33   John 15v1-2   Galatians 5v22

Fruit bushes enjoy light. If they are cultivated under shady trees or in other dull areas, they will not produce fruit. If they are not fed they will not develop.

The Holy Spirit in your life will produce fruit. Do you tend to block the production of fruit in your life? You will need the light of God's light to shine forth, and you will need to feed on the Word of God in order to develop. Each one of us has been given a particular gift or 'fruit' and it is our responsibility to help develop that gift and use it for the blessing of others and for the glory of God.

PRAYER – Father, I rejoice in the gift You have bestowed upon me. Thank you for Your light which will help me to grow, and the power of Your Word and Your Spirit which will help me to develop.

NOVEMBER 20th

Psalm 56v3-4   Isaiah 43v2-3   Matthew 17v20-21

If house windows are left open during the summer, it is not unusual for a bird to fly in. To watch that poor little bird rushing about and bumping into things, paints a perfect picture of frustration. You try to help but the bird is too 'strung up' to respond.

Are there times in your life when you get so frustrated that you spend your time rushing about, bumping into one problem after another? Stop for a moment and think. In His Word, God promises time and time again that impossible situations will not get the better of you. Listen to Him and act accordingly. What a wonderful promise. Remember too, that through all the uncertainty ahead, Jesus is just beside you.

PRAYER – Father, I get such a feeling of peace and security when I know You can control my feelings of frustration. Thank you for Your assurance and comforting encouragement. Help me to listen and respond.

NOVEMBER 21st

Psalm 61v1-2   Romans 7v22-25   Colossians 1v13-14

It is not unusual for any of us to do exactly what we have been told not to do. If instructions are clear this should not be a problem, but sometimes we simply do not listen, so we don't know any better than to do what we think is right.

Do you spend a dedicated time each day reading God's Word and listening to what He has to say? According to your behaviour, you should marvel that God is so loving with you. Rest back awhile and hear what God is saying; it is so important, then you won't make mistakes, or be disobedient to God's desire for your life.

PRAYER – Father, please hear my cry for forgiveness. I am so sorry that I have not always listened to You and have therefore made mistakes because of my disobedience.

NOVEMBER 22nd

Psalm 18v28   John 1v4-5   1Peter 2v9

Country lanes can be very dark at night when there is no moon to light up the way. How do you know where to go if you cannot see?

Do you become frustrated when times are hard or uncertain in your Christian life and the way is dark? You have to learn to be patient and accept the Holy Spirit in your life to take control. 'Feel' through God's Word and you will be guided through the darkness as He leads you in the right direction. You will be encouraged and long to praise Him for His love and care.

PRAYER – Father, please guide me through the darkness of my thinking and help me along the right way. Thank you for Your loving concern in showing me where to go.

NOVEMBER 23rd

Exodus 14v13-14   Matthew 14v27   Luke 8v22-25

The weather can be very disturbing sometimes, especially when a storm develops. The wind will increase and often it is so strong that it is impossible to stand. We have to cling to something solid in order to avoid being blown over.

How near are you to Jesus when the storms blow? It is wonderful to know that Jesus is so near to you and that whatever happens, His love supports and surrounds you. He will take care of you in every situation, like a strong 'pole' which you can cling to as the 'winds' seem to blow you over. Have no fear, have no doubts and through the grace of God, get to the stage of complete trust, confidence and peace in Jesus.

PRAYER – Father, there are times when I need to have some firm support as the storm clouds gather. Thank you that You sent Jesus to be my constant support.

NOVEMBER 24th

Joshua 1v8-9   Jeremiah 7v23-24   Hebrews 11v8-10

Everyone has certain desires in life and will make plans to fulfil those desires. Then somehow the novelty wears off and progress is made no further. They never really get started.

Do you have any ambitions to develop your Christian life? You will need to have commitment to that ambition and get going. Don't make excuses but be consistent in all you do, or you will never reach the goal. There will be 'hiccups' but just take one step at a time and tackle each 'hiccup' as you get to it. Pray that God will take you in the right direction. But you must faithfully follow His instructions, never wandering or hesitating. You will get there in the end.

PRAYER – Father, I have great desires and plans in my life but rely upon Your constant guidance as I commit myself to go forward. Don't let me give up now that my mind is made up.

NOVEMBER 25th

Matthew 6v19-21   Philippians 4v19   Colossians2v2-3

When packing cases for holiday, it is so easy to take far more than is really necessary. The problem arises when we have to transport more luggage than we need. Then when we arrive, we soon realise the futility of packing so much that is not really necessary.

It is not necessary or right to yearn for more than you need in your pilgrim walk. Do you tend to long for certain things you do not have? Is the longing really necessary? You only need what is really necessary for your life here on earth and Jesus knows the essential needs. If you are truly committed to Him, He will make those clear to you. Without His guidance you would soon be in trouble, so don't rush to obtain unnecessary 'clutter' but trust in the Lord with all your heart and lean not unto your own understanding.

PRAYER – Father, don't let my desires run away with me. You know what I need and if I listen to You, I will be perfectly satisfied with what You enable me to have.

NOVEMBER 26th

Matthew 11v28-30   Mark 6v30-31   Hebrews 4v8-11

Step inside a busy office and watch what is going on. Everyone seems to be deeply involved, either glued to computers, running messages, answering phones and generally having no time to even notice you, let alone to ask you what you are there for. Totally committed to being busy.

Do you rest from time to time, or do you just keep going? To ignore the need for a rest, a break or a holiday, is to miss out, wear out and finish up in a state of frenzied confusion. It is not wrong to work hard, but do not ignore the need to hear the Lord speaking and this you can only do properly by listening. You need to keep fit and useful, so you need to be refreshed from time to time, then return to your particular task or ministry refreshed and ready to go.

PRAYER – Father, there always seems to be so much to do and I get overwhelmed and tired. Please help me to be sensible, to stop and relax and get refreshed so that I can be more useful in Your service.

NOVEMBER 27th

Romans 8v35-39   2Corinthians 4v6-10   1Peter 4v12-13

So many people, particularly in their latter years, suffer from painful physical conditions that can only be relieved by medication or various aids. The pain acts as a barrier to them, cutting them off from many activities in their lives.

It is not difficult to draw near to God, but then certain barriers tend to separate our contact with God. Do you have any barriers in your life? If pain is the barrier, think how much pain Jesus suffered to enable you to enter into the very presence of God. You will think back to Calvary and now Jesus will mean so much more to you because you have shared a little in His suffering. Let His love shine through your barrier and seek direction, comfort and release through God's Holy Word.

PRAYER – Father, I know that barriers tend to block my direct way to You, but through Your Word I seek help. Thank you for the wonderful example of Jesus to encourage me.

NOVEMBER 28th

Romans 6v12-14   1John 1v8-10   1John 4v13-16

Moving house can cause a great deal of stress. There is much clearing out to do, and items to be disposed of. The new house is too small for all the contents of the old house. Then a good clean up of dirt you did not know was there. But how good and rewarding is the outcome.

When did you last have a good sort out and clean up of your life? There is always a lot of this to do. Cleaning up and correction is so important. As you 'sift' through your life you will discover 'dirt' you did not know was there, but once you have sorted it all out, through prayer and a close relationship with Jesus, then you will be ready to witness for Him and let the love of God penetrate into new areas in the coming days.

PRAYER – Father, please help me as I examine my own life and sort out all the items that need to be cleared out and cleaned up. Thank you that Jesus will be my Guide.

NOVEMBER 29th

1Chronicles 28v20   John 12v26   Colossians 3v23-24

To take on a specific task means committing ones self to it, realising that this is your responsibility. To do it properly, you need to be faithful and not mind any effort that is necessary to make the task successful.

God's love is so wonderful that He will satisfy your longings. This will not last unless you remain faithful. Are you faithful doing the task God has asked you to do? The satisfaction He gives should be revealed in the love you show for the task you are doing. Your faith must be a believing faith, even when the Lord leads you through experiences you do not always understand. You have a responsibility to serve the Lord in the particular task He has called you to do.

PRAYER – Father, I have a task to do and I want to do it faithfully for Jesus. Thank you for opening up the way for me. Help me to realise my responsibilities.

NOVEMBER 30th

Isaiah 1v19   Hebrews 5v8-9   1Peter 1v13-16

Travelling along quiet roads or busy main roads, we have to watch the speed signs and cameras. If we go at a speed slightly over the limit allowed, we will receive a warning and a fine from the police. It is necessary to be obedient.

Is obedience of great importance for you in your Christian life? You should be willing to do what God asks you to do, then His love will be able to penetrate through. If you ignore His requests and instructions you will have to receive the consequences and be prepared for correction. Always be alert, then whatever happens, you can be quite sure that you will learn something from it.

PRAYER – Father, I am perfectly capable of making mistakes and of disobedience. Please help me to be alert and ready for all You want to teach me.

DECEMBER

DECEMBER 1st

Psalm 61v2-4   Psalm 121v5   Isaiah 40v29

Animal charities do a wonderful work. They rescue animals and birds from appalling situations and sometimes find them in a state of exhaustion. They treat the sick ones and try to encourage others, with care, love and concern. They cannot speak but they do respond.

Do you realise that God overrules every situation you are in, or feelings you may have? When you feel tired or exhausted, God understands and will give you any necessary strength when you feel you can no longer cope. Jesus will open the way for you to rest in the presence of God. Come close to Him and discover how much He loves you. Then you will have cause to rejoice and be glad.

PRAYER – Father, I was at my wits end when you found me, but now as I rest in Your care, I feel the warmth of Your love and my heart is just full of praise.

DECEMBER 2nd

Matthew 21v21-22   Romans 8v26-27   1John 2v26-27

These days we are confronted with a variety of alternative medicines and natural products designed to help and to relieve certain medical problems. It is natural to have doubts about these products.

Do you sometimes have doubts about certain thoughts, feelings, ideas or notions? You sometimes wonder whether God is speaking or whether you are planning and scheming yourself. Hand over your doubts to the Lord and ask Him to make your thinking clear. Then it doesn't matter what anyone tries to say, because the Lord is now in control and will cause you to react and respond through the power and direction of His Spirit.

PRAYER – Father, I do have doubts sometimes and I need the guidance of the Holy Spirit in my life to make the way clear. Thank you again that Jesus is always ready and willing to reveal Your love.

DECEMBER 3rd

Genesis 18v13-14   Isaiah 65v24   1Peter 5v7

Fathers have a great responsibility. Whether he has one or a dozen children, he needs to care for their well being. They in return, should appreciate their father, but this is not always the case. There is sometimes abuse by the father and there maybe children's rejection.

Is your whole life wrapped up in God? Do you realise that all your concerns are His concerns? God is completely involved in the affairs of all His children; all at the same time, although it is quite impossible for us to understand how this works. He also has everything mapped out ahead, but you must spend time keeping in constant touch.

PRAYER – Father, I just praise and thank you for the fact that You care for all of us every day and plan our future. It is wonderful and I am so grateful.

DECEMBER 4th

2Samuel 22v29   2Corinthians 5v7   1Peter 2v9

Night follows day every 24 hours, but it is not in the same place at the same time because the world is continually revolving.

Life is one long story of light and darkness; one always follows the other. Do you experience many dark nights in your life? God is in control and in time, night becomes day providing you put your trust in Him. You do not have to see, only believe and you will have the wonderful experience of 'seeing the light at the end of the tunnel.' Have faith that believes and appreciates, faith that is positive, and night will no longer hold the fear it had. The daytime results will prove it.

PRAYER – Father, I do tend to get lonely sometimes in the night, but thank you that I can look forward to the sunshine of daytime and know that faith works.

DECEMBER 5th

Romans 5v3-5   2Corinthians 12v9-10   James 1v2-4

Did you ever realise how much the touch of a hand means to someone; a sick or unhappy child or a lonely person? It indicates concern and love; a sign of warmth and comfort.

If you never felt the hand of God upon you sometimes in the form of punishment or correction, you would have reason to think that God no longer had any interest in you. Have you ever experienced the feeling of God's hand upon you? He is interested and He does love you, otherwise He would not be so concerned. Suffering for instance, just brings you nearer to Him because you long for His love and comfort. All the experiences through which you pass should help. Consider others as God considers you and make them feel loved by your touch of encouragement.

PRAYER – Father, I need to lean more upon You as You touch me with Your hand of love and concern. I will be so much closer to You than if I try to stand alone.

DECEMBER 6th

Genesis 3v1-7   Matthew 26v41   Romans 7v22-25

Generally speaking people want to do what is right, but there is something in human nature that tries to encourage us to do the opposite. It is when we give in, that trouble results. There seems to be a lot of 'giving in' in our world today.

Are you constantly confronted with that feeling of being drawn away from what you know to be right? You will have a feeling that you need to be 'wrapped up' in God, so that you can only do what is right. It is so easy for the 'wrap' to become unfolded slightly, and for sinful thoughts to creep in. Be deeply involved in Jesus and be conscious of His overpowering Spirit and love. Keep faithful and 'afloat' with praise.

PRAYER – Father, I do need to feel the comfort and encouragement of Your loving arms always surrounding me. I need the presence of Jesus in my life. Please help me to concentrate upon these important matters.

DECEMBER 7th

2Corinthians 5v21   Romans 8v29-30   Titus 3v3-7

A plain piece of material can appear very ordinary until a skilled embroiderer gets to work. Small sections will be removed and then attractive designs and elaborate silks etc, will make it so much more attractive.

When sin is removed from your life there will be a vacuum. Now Jesus can get to work. Do you notice the difference when Jesus comes into your life? It is a tremendous thought to realise that Jesus went through pain and humiliation to save us, in order that we might enter the Kingdom of God. He never complained or tried to avoid suffering. So He will care for you and you have no cause to be anxious. As more 'sections' are removed from your life, fill them with the love of Jesus and bring pleasure to others.

PRAYER – Father, please help me to be willing to have my life transformed according to Your will and purpose. Keep me trusting You.

DECEMBER 8th

Luke 2v8-20   John 3v16   2Corinthians 9v15

As the Christmas season begins to appear through the Advent season, we sense the true meaning of this time of the year. At the same time, we think about our friends and family and join in the excitement of 'What to give them for Christmas?'

Are you beginning to prepare for Christmas and have you organised your 'gift' list? As you have the love of Jesus is your heart, you just have to love other people too. Take delight in their success stories and don't be envious. If they have love for you too, then there will be a free flow. But if not, don't give up but take advantage of the opportunity God has given you, to show compassion if this is necessary. Understand the importance of a loving concern.

PRAYER – Father, take me as I am and help me to enter into the spirit of Christmas; a time of loving fellowship and witness within a troubled world.

DECEMBER 9th

John 14v1-4   2Peter 3v8-12a   Revelation 22v20-21

When one expects an important visitor, an urgent house cleaning and tidy up takes place. Then there are doubts about the time of the visitor's arrival, so we 'slow up.' We want to know the time so that we can be ready.

There are no doubts in the Bible that Jesus will be returning to planet earth; that is a certainty. Do you have any doubts about His return? As you think about it, pray and turn to the many references in Scripture and believe what you learn. Get excited and realise the responsibility you have to alert others. You will not just 'tidy up' and prepare, then sit and wait. You must carry on as normal, but the important point is to make sure you are ready for that wonderful day when Jesus will return.

PRAYER – Father, I want to be ready when Jesus returns and I want to alert others too. I rejoice as I prepare for that great day.

DECEMBER 10th

Psalm 91v14-16   Romans 8v37-39   2Thessalonians 2v16-17

So many people in the world are in refugee situations, many are homeless and unprotected from stormy and cold weather and have no shelter during the cold nights.

Do you realise that the love of God is wrapped around you like a thick blanket? You are completely protected from outside elements. Christ's suffering and death released that blanket of love, which provides comfort, peace and joy, all rolled into one. Now think of so many who do not know that blanket and suffer from so many outside elements of fear, sadness and hardships. You will want to share some of the comfort with them and pray that they too, may experience and accept all that God offers to them.

PRAYER – Father, what a privilege it is to enjoy Your wonderful blanket of love. I long that others too will share this excellent gift, and experience Your peace.

DECEMBER 11th

Psalm 34v5   Isaiah 58v8   Daniel 12v3

Electric radiators are so useful during the winter months, especially the ones that can be moved around. But if the radiator is not connected to the electricity plug, then no heat will come out of the radiator because there is no power.

Do you long to radiate the love of Jesus to your friends and contacts? In order for this to happen you need to be 'switched on' to the main source of supply; Jesus. If you do not, the warmth of His love will not shine through your life to effect other people. There must be a regular check through your life to make sure that everything is in working order, then let love flow without interference.

PRAYER – Father, I want Your love to flow through my life. Then I can be a comfort and encouragement to others. Please encourage me to 'switch on' to Your power.

DECEMBER 12th

Psalm 27v14   Isaiah 41v10   1Corinthians 16v13

Out in the countryside we love to explore the exciting paths through the forest or across the moors. Sometimes the main path is not always clear and as we scramble over various objects, we wonder if we are on the right track.

The Lord never promised a smooth passage through life. How often do you come up against obstacles in the way, and what do you do about them? The enemy is always around and there are battles to fight. There are disappointments, fears, anxieties, problems, trouble, pain, sorrow and trials. How do you possibly cope with all these things and stay pure and faithful to the Lord? You must increase your faith and spend more time in prayer and Bible study. Here you will find courage and victory and the right track to follow.

PRAYER – Father, I must not lose heart but rejoice in the fact that You will uphold me and give me the determination to 'press on.' Thank you, Lord.

DECEMBER 13th

Colossians 1v10-12   Colossians 2v6-7   2 Peter 3v18

All plants and trees have roots. These are the main source of nourishment intake. It is necessary for the soil to be moist and full of goodness in order for the plants to grow and develop.

The roots of your faith need to go deep into the soil of God's love. When this happens, you will be conscious of a spiritual growth that you did not have before. Are you conscious of a new development in your faith as you penetrate 'roots' into the 'soil' of God's love? Water the 'soil' in prayer, then soak up His Word and really feel the power of God's strength rising up into your life. If you continue to do this, His love will overflow to reveal the praise and glory of the Lord.

PRAYER – Father, as I soak up all the goodness from the soil of Your love, help me to develop and grow in my faith and witness amongst my colleagues and family, I pray.

DECEMBER 14th

Deuteronomy 31v7-8   Isaiah 65v24   Luke 22v41-44

Tornados develop during hurricane storms. Anything caught in the middle of one of these is torn from its foundations with great force. You can rarely detect their arrival. The tornado is followed by a great clear up.

Rough patches or 'tornados' are not uncommon during our Christian pilgrimage. Have you had any 'rough weather' lately? Now the way is far from smooth but as a Christian you are not alone, even if you feel that way. You really want to call upon the Lord when you are involved in 'rough weather.' Jesus experienced this when He cried to His Father in the Garden of Gethsemane where He agonised so greatly. You share in Christ's suffering in times like this. It seems difficult, but Jesus will lift you up as the Holy Spirit encourages you.

PRAYER – Father, I do not enjoy going through 'tornados' having my life disrupted and disturbed, but thank you that You understand. I praise You, Father.

DECEMBER 15th

Galatians 6v2   Philippians 2v4-5   1Peter 3v8

When we have problems, difficult situations or important decisions to make, a natural reaction is to share with someone who can help or advise. On the other hand, we may long to help someone who is going through a problem time.

Are you in a situation when you want to help and advise someone who is having problems? You should be so one with God that your one desire is to love people, otherwise you are just ignoring Him. Jesus spent His time giving Himself to people. It would be good if you would have a burden for people and really be involved in their interests and so reveal God's love to them through your actions.

PRAYER – Father, may my concern for my friends reveal Your concern for them too. Give me the words to speak that will bring comfort and encouragement to them.

DECEMBER 16th

Acts 9v5-6   Ephesians 6v18   Philippians 4v6-7

When folks are up against problems too big for them to tackle, they tend to turn to prayer and plead to God. They do not really know God any way, only that He exists somewhere and is, as it were, a last resort.

Do you consider prayer as a direct contact with a living God? You must be sincere and confident when you pray and be thankful for what you have already received from Him. Intercede for others and hand all the details to God in faith, believing that He will take control and already has the answer planned. Let God work out His purposes as you pray a prayer of commitment and consecration. God will then be able to work out His purposes through you as you trust in Him.

PRAYER – Father, take me as I am and work out Your purposes through me. I come to You, confident that my prayers will be answered in Your time.

DECEMBER 17th

Psalm 51v10-11   Acts 2v17-18   Romans 8v26-27

If water is poured into a container that has a small puncture in the base, the water will slowly leak through the puncture and the water level in the container will slowly drop.

Your Christian life comes alive when the Holy Spirit fills you with all the necessary qualities. If your life has a 'leak' the Spirit will drop and need to be 'topped up.' Are you conscious of any 'leaks' in your Christian life? You have a wonderful future of eternal life ahead, but you need to be continually filled with a fresh anointing of the Holy Spirit day by day. Then what ever events you experience, learn to praise the Lord. Read the Word, pray and rejoice in the Lord always.

PRAYER – Father, I rejoice in You and will accept every experience according to Your will. May the power of Your presence in my life block any 'leaks' and enable the Spirit in my life give me enthusiasm to serve You every day.

DECEMBER 18th

John 14v13-14   Philippians 4v6   James 1v5

As Christmas draws near, we consider gifts that we plan to give to family and friends. The children usually produce lists of requests that they hope to have and we try to oblige if at all possible.

When you come to the Lord with a particular request, do you believe that you will receive what you ask for? The Lord does not always give you what ever you ask for, but if you ask Him about your request, He will give you the wisdom you need to make the right decision. Always pray for wisdom and guidance before asking God for anything, then you will not be disappointed if He makes it clear that the request was your own desire, not His.

PRAYER – Father, thank you that You know better than me what I really need. I'm sorry that I get such bright ideas, but thank you for the wisdom you give me to make the right decisions.

DECEMBER 19th

Isaiah 50v10   2Corinthians 12v9   Hebrews 4v15-16

Many nativity plays will now be in action and many children will be excited about the parts they have to play. They will be impatient and often nervous. Teachers and leaders too will experience a little tension and sometimes a feeling of weakness that everything will go well.

Are you experiencing moments of weakness if you have a special part to play over Christmas? It may be entertaining and there is so much to do in preparation; shopping and cooking etc. It is a real comfort to know that Jesus understands your weaknesses and knows how you feel. There may be some dark patches to come, but the light of the Lord will encourage you, so do not despair. Be patient and confident, trust in the Lord and everything will happen as it should.

PRAYER – Father, this is an exciting time of the year as we consider the wonderful story of the birth of Your dear Son and all that it means to us, Your people. I praise You for the wonder of it all.

DECEMBER 20th

Genesis 1v14-16   Psalm 18v28   John 1v4-5

Although the nights are now dark and cold, bright lights are shining everywhere; street lights and coloured lights in the shop windows. They all brighten up the darkness and cause us to feel so much better.

Some folk prefer to walk in darkness and complain about the lights anyway! Which way do you chose to go and do you spend a lot of time complaining? God has chosen you for a specific task and although you like the bright lights, it maybe that you have to walk in darkness sometimes. Faith cannot grow without hardship, so that is why you sometimes have to go through the darkness. God had plans for you all along, but you probably knew nothing about them. Do not despair. God will bring light out of your darkness when He is ready.

PRAYER – Father, I do not enjoy the darkness and I look forward to the bright lights that I will experience as You lead me on.

DECEMBER 21st

Nahum 1v7   John 16v33   2Corinthians 5v4-7

To be confronted with the thought of having an operation is not an attraction that encourages us. But when pain is involved, an operation to cure the trouble is acceptable and the resulting relief is worth the previous pain.

What a tremendous future you have to look forward to. No pain, no anxieties and no troubles. Do you get excited just thinking about it and do surrounding problems seem to be less of a trouble? Without this assurance and the continual guidance of Jesus, life would be so different. It would be one continual round of doubts and fears with no prospects of a solution. Jesus will support you as problems and 'pains' are dealt with and will lead you nearer to that heavenly home where there will be continual joy, peace and love.

PRAYER – Father, no one enjoys suffering pain but I thank you that You have made a way for a cure and it is so wonderful to be able to experience the relief that it gives.

DECEMBER 22nd

1Corinthians 13v1-7   Ephesians 2v10   1John 3v11

As Christmas draws nearer there is much evidence of special efforts to provide help and treats for so many areas where there are needs. This is a special time to help one another.

Love is the basis of everything in the Christian life. Do you have a special feeling of love for everyone at this time of the year? Be like Jesus in your reaction to other people. Your priority is to have faith in God and in the fact that His love will be translated into action, in your reaction to other people. It is so wonderful to know that Jesus was sent by God, to create in us this wonderful love. What exciting fellowship we can have together if our love for one another is God's love flowing through us. Jesus came as a baby but as He grew and developed, so did His love.

PRAYER – Father, thank you for Jesus and His love which penetrates into my heart and gives me a wonderful longing to love those with whom I come into contact each day.

DECEMBER 23rd

Psalm 26v3   John 14v27   Romans 5v1-2

We are aware of a wonderful picture of peace as we picture the Baby Jesus lying so lovingly in the manger. It makes peace so very real.

The peace of God which Jesus brings is an incredible peace that can wrap itself around you in such a way that you will have no fears or anxieties, but just feel full of love. Have you experienced that wonderful peace? You can only obtain it through complete dedication to Jesus. What a privilege it is to be able to understand the true meaning of Christmas as we adore the Babe at Bethlehem.

PRAYER – Father, may Your peace transform my thinking as I consider the birth of Your Son, Jesus. I worship and adore You in Your concern for us all, in sending Jesus.

DECEMBER 24th

Psalm 95v6-7   Matthew 2v10-11   Luke 2v8-18

As we picture the shepherds on the hillside outside Bethlehem, we can imagine their surprise and alarm as the Angel announced the arrival of Jesus. We see them hasten to the stable. We enter the excitement.

Are you stirred by the Christmas massage and do you relate to all the people concerned? As Christian people, we understand the story as it is revealed in Scripture. Call to all who listen as you proclaim the love of Jesus wherever you go. Come as you are, as the shepherds did, leaving their duties to worship the new born King. Do not let other things take the place of your responsibilities. Worship the Lord in the beauty of holiness and be encouraged.

PRAYER – Father, I can never thank you enough for sending Jesus. As a Babe, we worship and adore Him. He means so much to me in my walk with You.

DECEMBER 25th

Isaiah 9v6   Matthew 1v22-23   Luke 2v4-7

On this very special day we sing triumphantly 'Come and behold Him, born the King of angels, come adore Him, Christ the Lord.'

How much do you sing and praise Jesus as He came to us in such simplicity? This is the goodness of God in letting His Son come to live amongst us in order to open up the way for us to come into the presence of God, Himself. Take time to celebrate this great occasion. Meet with God's people in joyful celebration. Consider what the life of Jesus has meant to you and share your experience with everyone you meet. Share the Scriptures and bring them to the notice of any who do not realise what Christmas really means.

PRAYER – Father, thank you for making this day possible. Thank you that You want to save Your people and You have sent Jesus to make this possible through His life and witness amongst us.

DECEMBER 26th

Matthew 2v1-12   2Corinthians 4v4-6   1John 4v14-15

Three kings came to see and worship Jesus, the new King, but they had really been sent to 'spy out' the situation and were requested to return to King Herod to report to him what they had seen.

Are you conscious of folk being only vaguely interested when you try to share the true meaning of the Christmas story? Do not be despondent because there will always be those who try to ridicule or who try to disillusion you when you mention Christian activities. Your faith must remain firm and positive as you trust the truth of God's Word and seek to follow the instructions and encouragement you find there. There will always be those who have doubts and we all have a responsibility to share the truth with them.

PRAYER – Father, I do pray that You will enable me to draw folk to You through the Christmas season as I seek to reveal the true meaning of this wonderful time.

DECEMBER 27th

Psalm 32v7-8   Psalm 61v1-5   1Peter 5v8-9

Wild animals are always on the alert because predators are always ready to attack them. As soon as there is a warning, they race for cover.

Are you always on the alert to check your way of life and make sure you are following God's way for you? It is necessary for you to respond to any warning you may have, and always keep in touch with the Lord. He will warn you when danger is near and you must obey His call. Never rely on yourself but rejoice and be thankful for His loving care.

PRAYER – Father, keep me close beside You as I seek to follow the way You have called me. I need to be alert and ready to respond when You call.

DECEMBER 28th

Psalm 95v6   Isaiah 26v3-4   Hebrews 12v1

In the midst of all the seasonal activities, daily routines have to continue. Meals need to be prepared, children cared for, housework, shopping, business and a host of other routine activities. All must be attended to accordingly.

Have you realised how important it is to remember that despite all that involves you, Jesus should be your main consideration? Born a King, in a humble stable setting, He came to be the Saviour of the world. Now, as you consider the excitement of His arrival, come aside from your busy routine and worship Him. In the seasonal atmosphere, you have the wonderful opportunity of being able to share the true meaning of Christmas by your reaction to all that is happening.

PRAYER – Father, What a wonderful time of the year this is as I concentrate on the birth of Jesus and what this meant as He grew and developed as You had planned, to witness and save all who turn to Him.

DECEMBER 29th

Isaiah 30v15   Romans 15v5-6   1Thessalonians 5v14-18

There is always a weight limit with our luggage when we travel by air. Should the plane be overloaded it will face difficulties and may even crash.

Do you sometimes feel that you are overloaded by the cares of this world and the cares of other people? You try to help folk with their problems and because you are co-operative, they know to whom they can turn. But take care, because if you try to overload yourself with everyone's problems, you may run into difficulties yourself. Don't take on too much or you will never reach the heights of God's plan for you and you may even crash, because you ignore your limitations. So set a limit and 'fly' well, then you will be a help to the folk you want to help and a blessing to God in His service.

PRAYER – Father, So many folk need help and guidance as they consider the reasons Jesus came, and the significance that this time of the year means. Help me to be useful but to know my limitations.

DECEMBER 30th

1Chronicles 28v20   Joshua 1v7-9   Psalm 90v1-2

Parties and entertainment seem to be the order of the day as we end the year. These involve a great deal of preparation and planning.

At the end of the year do you begin to think about your plans for next year? Now is the time to celebrate God's goodness, protection and provision for the past year and rejoice in celebration as you think back to all He has meant to you over the year. Do not dwell upon the incidents that have been 'down' moments but thank God for the 'up' times. You have just been celebrating the arrival of Jesus, and realising how much He has changed your life as you have accepted His Spirit to guide you into another year.

PRAYER – Father, thank you for all You have meant to me throughout the past year. I place myself into Your loving hands for the year ahead.

1Samuel 7v12   Isaiah 41v13   Hebrews 13v5-6

On the last day of the year we tend to think back over the past year. Experiences, things not done or things done. It's like looking down a long avenue of trees, triumphs and temptations all the way.

Are you thinking about your experiences of the past year? What did those experiences mean to you? Are you able to claim that 'Hitherto has the Lord helped me?' Now is the time to look forward. There are still distances to be covered, with more trials, temptations and triumphs. Do not let barriers build up with discontent, hatred and envy. Unite in fellowship, love one another and learn to forgive one another. Spend time in prayer for clear guidance ahead and spend time in the Word learning the way. 'He who hath helped thee hitherto will help thee all thy journey through.' [author unknown]

PRAYER – Father, it is true that you have helped me so much in the past, now I plead with you to help me in the future. I am confident that my prayer has been heard as I go forward, praising you that you have sent Jesus to guide me all the way.

OTHER BOOKS
BY THE SAME AUTHOR

Mwanza
Flying Forceps
Cheaper by the Million
Lifeline to Millions
Children's Bible story painting books
Challenged to Conquer (autobiography)
Born to Serve (autobiography)
Tales from the Congo Forest
Daily Walks in the Forest
Jungle Nurse

KING'S HIGHWAY SERIES
Commandments for Travellers
Promises for Travellers
Search the Scriptures
Led by the Shepherd
Follow the Shepherd
Great Prayers of the Bible
Great Commandments of the Bible
Great Promises of the Bible

N/B   Some of the earlier books are now out of print.

———————